Dialogue
with My Sons

By Jeffrey A. Johnson, Sr.

PRESS

Cover Design by Tina Williams, Tru Essence Designs
www.truessencedesign.com

www.xulonpress.com

For my four beloved sons, in whom I am well pleased—J. Allen, Jordan, Jalon, and Josiah.

You know how much I love you, and how much I am enjoying getting to know the men you are becoming. My prayer for each of you, and for my sons in the faith, is that you will always seek God first in your life, live out the calling that God has for you, and remember who you are, and Whose you are.

Love,
Dad

Table of Contents

Foreword

By Michael Eric Dyson

A Critical Message for Black Males

One of the most important things you need to know about Jeffrey Johnson is that he's got the guts to say what needs to be said to today: Our success as black males is a matter of both our personal responsibility *and* the opportunities and obstacles we face in the world. That's a simple statement that shouldn't be controversial at all. Yet there's a huge line drawn in the sand between those who harp on personal responsibility like nothing else counts, and those who stress the impediments society throws in our way while ignoring that our fate is often in our own hands.

Thank God for Pastor Jeffrey Johnson. He is willing to tell black males that they need to get their acts together: that they must police their moral boundaries, develop a personal relationship with God, resist the temptation to make excuses for their failures, and build on the strong religious foundations developed by their ancestors.

But Pastor Johnson does not stop there. He also highlights the political, social, moral and racial obstacles that block opportunities for black men and that often prevent them from exercising their God-given abilities in our country. Pastor Johnson goes even further to highlight the lingering racism, persistent bigotry, ugly economic inequality and social stigma that dog the paths of too many black males.

Pastor Johnson is willing to empower the unjustly disempowered and to disempower the immorally powerful. In short, he is both a prophet and a priest. He takes measure of the social landscape and offers advice that keeps black males from sinking into victimhood while championing the upward striving of black males who face unfair barriers.

The dialogue you hold in your hand brims with wisdom, teems with knowledge, vibrates in compassion and explodes with theological insight as Pastor Johnson offers encouragement and uplift to young black males. After reading these pages, you'll know that you're in the presence of a loving but demanding sage. To hear Pastor Johnson preach in the pulpit is to witness a homiletical fury that distributes intellectual brilliance and poetic passion in its wake. But to read him on the page is to discern a wise elder at the height of his powers as he serves nuggets of truth and inspiration that nourish our spirits.

Pastor Johnson is one of the greatest examples of the lessons he teaches. He has weathered the storms of poverty, racism, illness, psychic trauma and social hardship to become one of the most gifted preachers, effective pastors and sharpest thinkers we have in the nation today. Pastor Johnson has yielded his poetic pen to disciplined reflection and penetrating analysis to help our young black males become better and greater men. This book and the man who wrote it are national treasures.

Michael Eric Dyson, Ph.D.
Georgetown University
Washington, D.C.

Introduction by Sharon Henry Johnson

Our Gifts from God

I t is my privilege to write the introduction to this book that my husband has written for our sons and for countless others who want to hear words of wisdom, insight, and advice from the heart of a loving father. In talking with me about this book, Jeffrey pointed out that he did not produce or parent our children by himself. He, therefore, wanted my voice to be heard as well. He has written this book as a father, but the mother's role is equally essential. So, for the boys, men, and other mothers who read this book, I offer this introduction as a backdrop for *Dialogue with My Sons.*

Psalm 127:3 (NLT) says, "Children are a gift from the LORD; they are a reward from him." When I think of our four sons, I recognize that they are gifts—very, very precious gifts—from God to my husband Jeffrey and me.

From the very moment that the doctor told me I was pregnant with each of our sons, I began praying for them, and never stopped!

I have prayed for them to become great men of God, men who will live for Him, honor Him, and always have a desire to serve Him. I have prayed for them to have good friends along the way, who would share their love for God and would join them in making good decisions and seeking the best for their lives. While none of our sons are yet married, I have been praying all along for them to choose godly wives who will be like the woman in Proverbs 31:11-12 (NIV): "Her husband has full confidence in her and lacks nothing of value. She brings him good, not harm, all the days of her life."

The Bible tells us to be good stewards over everything that He gives us. That includes our children. Being a parent is not just providing shelter, food, and clothing. Those things may help them to survive, but they also need additional things that will help them to live lives that have meaning, purpose, and joy. It is through reading to them from God's Word, instilling within them moral values, and teaching them godly principles that we have provided our sons with a foundation upon which they can grow lives that allow them to fulfill God's purposes for bringing them into this world.

As the woman with whom they spent the most time while they were growing up, it was my responsibility to set an example for them. This meant living out all of the things Jeffrey and I were teaching them. It means nothing if parents *tell* their children one thing, but *do* the opposite. I couldn't tell my sons to be kind to others and then be unkind myself. I couldn't tell them to let their talk please God and then let my own speech be filled with gossip or swearing. I couldn't tell them to put God first and then spend all of my time on entertainment, shopping, and living just for my own pleasure.

My lifestyle—how I lived, talked, drank, ate, and treated others—was continually teaching them how we, as Christians, live in this world. My actions spoke far louder than my words. Everything I did influenced them. Being a parent is a full-time relationship. It doesn't matter what setting we're in or what else we are doing, we are always parents.

Not only did our sons learn from me what "Mom" is like; they learned from me what a *woman* is like. By the way I dressed, the way I spoke, and the way I carried myself, I was constantly teaching them what a woman looks, dresses, acts, and speaks like. It is said that girls often look for qualities in a husband that they saw in their own fathers, and boys often look for qualities in their wives that they saw in their own mothers. That means that if I want my sons to find wives who look and behave as Christian women, I needed to model that before them as they were growing up. If I want them to marry women who will love God and love their families, I needed to show my sons what that type of woman looks like.

The women our sons marry will be the mothers of our grand-children. If we want our grandchildren to grow up in warm and loving homes, we need to be sure we are setting that example in our own homes, where *our* children are growing up. Our behavior and attitudes as parents will be handed down as a legacy throughout generations.

Children get their core identity from what their parents say to them. If a child is continually told he is stupid by either of his parents, he will grow up thinking he is stupid. If a child is told he is "good for nothing," he will grow up believing he is good for nothing. That is why it is so crucial to let our children know that they are good, kind, smart and beautiful and that they each have an important role to play in the family, in their school, in their church, in the community and in the world that no one else can fulfill. From the time our boys were little, I would tell them that they are intelligent. To be sure that they heard me, I would tell them to repeat back to me what I had just said about them. Even when they were so young that they couldn't pronounce "intelligent" correctly, they still understood that I was saying something good about them.

Of all that we taught our sons, the importance of family love and support was right at the top of the list. They learned that we love them when they are good, make wise choices, and do all the right things. And they also learned that we love them when they behave badly, and make poor choices, and seem to be doing all the wrong things. As caring parents, we disciplined them when they were disobedient, but never for a moment did we cease to love them. From us, they learned what God's unconditional love is like. They learned that love is part of our character and that it is constant. It is not given or withheld according to what they do. It is always present because that's what real love is like.

Sadly, as our children grow older, there are times when they will make mistakes and will make poor choices. We cannot always be there to say, "Do this. Don't do that" or, "Choose this, not that." Sometimes, even when they know to do the right thing, they will choose to do the wrong thing instead. There are times when a mother's heart is grieved and when a father's heart is in pain because of something their child (at any age) has done that does not reflect what that child learned at home.

But even in those times of challenge and difficulty, we need to do three things: 1) continue to love them; 2) continue to pray for them; and 3) rely on God's Word that tells us in Proverbs 22:6: "Start children off on the way they should go, and even when they are old they will not turn from it."

As our children grow, there are new challenges that face us at each new age. As each of our sons moved from infant to toddler, from toddler to preschool, and on to each new phase, I asked God to help me to be a good parent as that new period of life was unfolding. I know that my help comes from the Lord and that I need *His* wisdom and guidance if I am ever going to be able to wisely guide my children along a new path.

The very best thing a mother can do for her children is to choose their father well. Young women need to keep that in mind when they are deciding whether or not to marry a particular man. If a woman wants to have children, she should be asking herself if this man who says he loves her would also love their children and be a good father to them. If he is still a child himself—wanting her to take care of him, provide for him, and make him happy—he won't even make a good husband, let alone a good father.

When Jeffrey and I got married, he didn't have money, prestige, or many of the things by which this world measures success. But he was a man who loved God, a man who loved me and treated me with respect and gentleness, and a man who was obedient to God's call upon his life. He couldn't promise me a lot of material blessings, but he was a man of character and I knew that he would always love God, always love me, and always love any children whom God might choose to give us. Even as I had been endeavoring to become a woman of God, he had been learning how to be the man God wanted him to be. So we entered into marriage with a determination to make our marriage work and, when God blessed us with children, to be faithful to Him in loving, nurturing and caring for those little ones entrusted to us.

Early on, I recognized that how I treated their father would have a huge impact upon our sons. I honor my husband, and he honors me. Neither of us belittles or disrespects the other. Our sons have never been able to play one parent against the other. Our sons have always had the security of knowing that their parents love each other, as well as loving them.

One of the greatest joys I have is when I'm out alone with my sons and, without fail, they bring up their Dad. They may quote him, or tell a story about something he did, or even do impersonations of him. I see the love they have for their father, and I feel overjoyed. It warms my heart because God has given their father such a deep love for them and I see them reciprocating that love.

For years, Jeffrey has been there for them in so many ways, and now they are there for him as well. He has lived a godly life before them, and he has their respect. They know he is not perfect, but they know his heart is faithful to his God, his family, and to others who look to him for spiritual support and guidance. It is this man who now reaches out with *Dialogue with My Sons* to share with other men and boys what he has shared with our own sons, and who does so with a heart of love and a desire to see *all* men live the life that God has for them.

Preface

To All of My Readers

My purpose for writing this book is not to analyze the state of young males in America or simply restate the latest survey of the many that exist. My purpose is to speak to you as a father would speak to his sons within a healthy relationship. I grew up in the inner city area of the twelfth largest city in the United States. My father abandoned our family. My mother worked two jobs and raised four children alone. We lived in poverty and I attended public schools. I know some of the struggles and temptations you are facing. I have had thousand of conversations with my four biological sons and many of my spiritual sons in an attempt to help them overcome the painful realities of life and take advantage of the opportunities that exist in our times.

This is a dialogue because I don't want you to simply read through the book to get information. Instead, I want you to reflect on what you read. Interact with these ideas. Think about your own situation and what God might be saying to you personally. I pray that our dialogue will inform, inspire, and motivate you so that you may realize the destiny that God has for you. As an African American man, I understand the unique needs and challenges of young Black males in our society, so this book comes from that perspective. The principles presented here, however, are applicable for *anyone* wanting to experience a more meaningful, fulfilling life.

Even if you are an adult and never had a father who talked with you about anything positive, significant, practical, or spiritual, I pray that you will open your heart, your mind, and your life to receive this word from a father's heart to God's sons. Whatever your age and circumstances, it's not too late to experience what God has for you. You are not too low down. You have not sinned too much. You are not too poor. You are not too old. You are not forgotten. God loves you. God can do exceedingly and abundantly above all that you can ask, think, or imagine. (Ephesians 3:20) I hope and pray that you will join me in this dialogue, and let's see what God can, and will, do in YOUR life.

To Other Fathers

In no way is this book an attempt to take the place of the fathers who are operating in their children's lives. I know that there are millions of fathers living in their homes with their children, loving their wives, and providing for their families. Additionally, hundreds of thousands of fathers have sole custody of their children and are right there in their lives—teaching, training, and nurturing them. And then there are millions of fathers who don't have custody of their children, but who are still in their lives. They are there for their sons by loving them, caring for them, and providing for them so that they can move successfully from boyhood to manhood.

As a father of four sons myself, I am simply coming alongside to help open the doors of communication between you and your son as you read and talk about this book together, or to offer you some food for thought as you seek to help your son maneuver through this challenging course of life in the twenty-first century.

CHAPTER 1

Let Me Holla Atcha

My child, listen when your father corrects you.

Don't neglect your mother's instruction.

What you learn from them will crown you with grace

and be a chain of honor around your neck.

My child, if sinners entice you,

turn your back on them!

They may say, "Come and join us.

Let's hide and kill someone!

Just for fun, let's ambush the innocent!

Let's swallow them alive, like the grave;

let's swallow them whole, like those who go

down to the pit of death.

Think of the great things we'll get!

We'll fill our houses with all the stuff we take.

Come, throw in your lot with us;

we'll all share the loot."

My child, don't go along with them!

Stay far away from their paths.

They rush to commit evil deeds.

They hurry to commit murder.

If a bird sees a trap being set,

it knows to stay away.

But these people set an ambush for themselves;

they are trying to get themselves killed.

Such is the fate of all who are greedy for money;

it robs them of life.

Wisdom shouts in the streets.

She cries out in the public square.

Proverbs 1:8-20, NLT

Pressure Everywhere

The title of this chapter is taken from Proverbs 1:20: "Wisdom shouts in the streets." In other words, son, let me holla atcha. So many things every day seek to get your *attention*, with the *intention* of influencing your decisions and choices. Every day, there are thousands of advertisements with which you have to come to grips as they try to influence your attitude, your ambition, your activity, and even your spending habits. Somebody is always trying to speak to you—your mother or father, grandmother or grandfather, a teacher, counselor, professor, pastor, minister, Sunday school teacher, neighbor, coach, or friend. Whether it's a Republican, Democrat, Libertarian, or Independent, somebody is always trying to get through to you. Whether it's a get-rich-quick plan or a pyramid scheme, a drug dealer or a gang banger, peer pressure or some woman with whom you have no business being, someone is always trying to get through to you. People are trying to focus your direction and decide your destiny *for* you. There is always somebody trying to influence you—some who have your best interests at heart, and others who have more selfish motives.

But in the midst of all of that pressure, Solomon, the writer of Proverbs, says that wisdom is shouting to you, even in the streets. Wisdom is hollering out at you. Wisdom is seeking to get your attention. Why? Because you will never be successful, never be prosperous, and never get to the destiny God has for you without wisdom.

There Is a God for Real

So, where does this wisdom come from? It all starts with God. Proverbs 9:10 (NIV) says, "The fear of the Lord is the beginning of wisdom," or, as Proverbs 1:7 (NLT) puts it, "Fear of the Lord is the foundation of true knowledge." You've got to know that there is a God and acknowledge that God is real.

When I was growing up, the children in our family learned to pray at an early age. Before every meal we would pray, "Father, I thank You for what I am about to receive for the nourishment of my body. For Christ's sake, Amen." I still remember it after all these years. Every night, on my knees, I was instructed to pray, "Now I lay me down to sleep; I pray the Lord my soul to keep. If I should die before I wake, I pray the Lord my soul to take."

Through these prayers, my mother was seeking to make sure that I was God-conscious, that I was aware that there is a God somewhere. She knew if I was assured of that whenever difficulties, hardships, and painful times came along, I wouldn't turn to the wrong things. Instead, I would call on the God to whom I had learned to pray.

When Jesus was dying on the cross for your sins and mine, seven final sayings came from His mouth. One of those was, "Father, into your hands, I commit my spirit" (Luke 23:46). That utterance was not something Jesus thought of on the fly. Those words didn't just come into His head out of the blue. In those days, Jewish parents taught their children to pray, just as my mother had taught me. Just like I learned to simply pray, "Now I lay me down to sleep. . .," the children of Jesus' day learned the prayer, "Father, into your hands, I commit my spirit." So, during one of the most difficult, hurtful, and traumatic times in Jesus' life, He was able to recall that prayer from childhood. He knew that God was His Father, and He could put His life in God's hands.

I wonder what people do when they have no God-consciousness. Whom do they call on? Whom do they turn to? In whose hands do they place their lives when trouble and difficulty come? I am so thankful I am conscious of God. I believe that God is real and I believe that God hears and answers prayer.

God Isn't Hiding

Remember that it is the fear of God that is the beginning of wisdom. It begins with recognizing that God is real. In Romans 1:18-20, the apostle Paul writes:

> The wrath of God is being revealed from heaven against all the godlessness and wickedness of people, who suppress the truth by their wickedness, since what may be known about God is plain to them, because God has made it plain to them. For since the creation of the world God's invisible qualities—his eternal power and divine nature—have been clearly seen, being understood from what has been made, so that people are without excuse.

God has provided enough evidence that everybody should recognize that there is a God somewhere. Yet there are some who suppress that truth, and when you suppress the truth of God, all you've got left is a lie. God says we are without excuse. In other words, we can't say, "I didn't know there's a God." Yes, we did. Nature itself speaks of the fact that God exists. When we look at the sun, the moon, the stars, the trees, the grass, the fish, the birds, other animals, and you and me, we know there's a God somewhere.

Nature Speaks

Nature testifies to the power of God because it took Somebody with power to put all of the universe together. This could be no accident. It's not the result of the big bang theory. Particles floating around in the universe randomly crashing into each other didn't create this universe and all that is in it. No, there's too much rational order for all this to be an accident.

This creation speaks not only of the power of God, but also of the wisdom of God. God had to be wise. Why do I say that? Look at the order in the universe. The sun rises in the east and sets in the west; it never rises in the west and sets in the east. This earth's rotation occurs during a twenty-four hour period and is so accurate that we can track the time of day, the month, and the year by its cycle. There's order in this.

Moreover, the sun is ninety-three million miles away from the earth. If the sun were located any closer, the earth would burn up. If it were placed any farther away, the earth would freeze. But since God is a God of wisdom, He put it in just the right place. Also, the moon is exactly where it's supposed to be. It influences the water in oceans, rivers, lakes, and streams. If the moon were located any closer to this earth, it would greatly affect the tides of the oceans, and much of the coastal land mass could even be submerged by great tsunamis. If there were no gravity in this world, everything would collapse. But, thankfully, God is a God of wisdom and order.

Thus, we have no excuse whatsoever for our unbelief. There is a God somewhere, for nature demonstrates His creative power. But some still say, "We don't believe in God because we don't see God," or "If we don't see God, we won't believe there is a God." There are a lot of things we don't see, but we know they're real. We don't see the wind, but we know it's real because we have evidence that it exists. There is an unseen reality. We cannot see it, but we've been given ample evidence to prove that it exists. That's how God is. We cannot see God, but we know there's a God somewhere because there is evidence that God exists.

When I was a child, my pastor would talk about the little boy who was at the park flying a kite. As he flew the kite, it went so high that it couldn't be seen any longer. An old man walked up to the boy and asked, "Boy, what are you doing?"

"I'm flying a kite."

The old man looked up and said, "I don't see one."

"No, but I'm still flying it."

"How do you know it's there? I don't see it."

"Every now and then I feel a little tug on the string."

No, I don't see God; but every now and then, I feel a little tug on the string of my heart. I know God is real. I believe that you feel a little tug at your heart sometimes, too, son. Not only does that mean that God exists, but it also means that He cares enough about you to try to get your attention.

Where Wisdom Begins

When the Bible says that the fear of God is the beginning of wisdom, it doesn't mean that we are to be frightened of God. It doesn't mean that we should be scared of God. The term "fear," as it is used here, means that we should reverence God. Deep respect for God is the beginning of wisdom. We should be in awe of God. The awe of God is the beginning of wisdom.

Sadly, some people say they believe in God, but they live as though there is no God. Our belief *in* God should lead us to a commitment *to* God. If we stop at simply a belief in God, we're no further along than the demons of hell. James 2:19 says, "You believe that there is one God. Good! Even the demons believe that—and shudder." Wisdom begins when we revere God—which means that we deeply respect, honor, praise, and worship Him—and then enter into a personal relationship with Him. In other words, we not only believe that Jesus died for our sins and rose again, but we respond by repenting of our sins and receiving Jesus Christ as our Savior and Lord.

Wisdom is not simply knowledge itself, but the application of that knowledge. If we have knowledge but don't apply it, that isn't wisdom; it's foolishness. Psalm 53:1 states clearly, "The fool says in his heart, 'There is no God.'" Perhaps an even bigger fool knows there is a God, but doesn't live like it.

One reason some of us do not apply godly knowledge to our lives is that we lack self-discipline. The latter part of Proverbs 1:7 (NLT) says, "Fools despise wisdom and discipline." A lot of people are living lives way below what God has planned for them because of a lack of self-discipline. They are missing the success, prosperity, and destiny that God has designed for them because they know what to do but choose not to do it. For us to say that we know the difference between right and wrong, good and evil, and truth and falsehood, yet choose not to make that application in our lives, is not wisdom but foolishness.

Discipline is in the same word family as "disciple." In Luke 9:23, Jesus said, "Whoever wants to be my disciple must deny themselves and take up their cross daily and follow me." He was saying that we need some discipline if we are going to be His disciple. That means that we listen to God and obey Him. God is the One who helps us to determine what is right and wrong. He helps us to know what is good and evil, and what is the truth and a lie. We can learn what God thinks by reading the Bible. It is the yardstick by which we measure everything else. So now, whenever I read or hear something, I check it out according to what the Word of God says.

Only God's Voice Matters

Everybody has something to say. Everybody has philosophies. Everybody has a point of view. So we can listen to them, but then we check it all out to see if it coincides with the Word. If it doesn't, then it's a lie. If it does, it is true. If we suppress the truth, all we've got left is a lie. We have to keep reading what God's Word says in order to have His wisdom to know the difference between right and wrong.

We don't know what is right and wrong, moral and immoral, based on surveys and polls. Just because a majority of people state in a survey that they believe something is right, that doesn't make it right. It's what God says that determines how true and just something is. If we live on the basis of what our family is saying, what our friends are saying, or what celebrities are saying, chances are good that we are going to be wrong. But when we read, listen to, and know the Word of God, we can walk in confidence that God will help us to walk uprightly.

When God created Adam and Eve, He put them in the garden and told them they could eat of every tree except one. He told them not to eat from it, or they would die. That was the tree of the knowledge of good and evil. Eating from this tree changed Adam and Eve's relationship with God. Before they disobeyed God, they listened to His voice, believing and obeying whatever He told them. If He said something was good, Adam and Eve thought it was good. If He said something was evil, Adam and Eve avoided it because they knew it was evil. It was so simple.

But after Adam and Eve disobeyed God, they no longer went to Him to ask about what was good and evil. Instead, they began trying to determine it for themselves. And they often ended up doing that which was evil because, in their own eyes, it seemed right. We have to get back to depending on God's wisdom as expressed through God's Word. We can't know right from wrong without Him.

Truth Is Absolute, Not Situational

There are times when something may be legal, but is still not ethical. There is a school of thought that is called situational ethics. Some people believe that we determine what is right and wrong based on the situation in which we find ourselves. This means that something may be right at one time but wrong at another time, depending on our situation.

Let me put this in context. My youngest son, K.J., said that he and his friends were having a conversation about ethics. The question came up, "Is it ever right to steal a Bible?" A situational ethicist might reason it out this way: "God wants me to have a Bible, but I have no money to buy one. So, if I steal a Bible, it's okay because of the situation I am in." Situational ethics can mess us up. If we reason things out in our own minds rather than doing what the Word of God says, we can make decisions that sound good to us, but are an affront to the God we serve.

For instance, if we believe in situational ethics, we might be able to reason with ourselves that it is okay to have sex outside of marriage and to live with someone without being married. Our thought process might go like this: "We can't afford to get married right now, but we're going to get married someday, so it's okay for us to go ahead and have sex now because of our situation. And God knows our hearts." Yes, God knows our hearts, and He knows whether we are willing to obey Him even when it doesn't feel good, even when it is not convenient, and even when it costs us something.

The Word of God teaches us that there is absolute truth. Some things are absolutely wrong, and some things are absolutely right, regardless of the circumstances. We must have enough faith and trust in God to know that, no matter what our circumstances, He is going to take care of us. If God wants us to have a Bible, He can provide one without our stealing it. If God wants us to be married, He can provide financially so that we can afford to do so—and He can help us maintain our sexual purity until the time we are married. It will be easier if we obey 2 Timothy 2:22 (KJV): "Flee also youthful lusts." This means, son, whenever you feel you may be getting into a compromising situation, RUN! Don't think about it or try to reason it through. Just run!

This principle of trusting God holds true in other areas as well. If I am hungry, God can provide food for me. Psalm 37:25 says, "I was young and now I am old, yet I have never seen the righteous forsaken or their children begging bread." If I need a job, money for rent, or clothes for my children, I don't have to hit someone upside the head and steal what that person has worked to earn. I can go to my God because, as Philippians 4:19 says, "And my God will meet all your needs according to the riches of his glory in Christ Jesus." That doesn't say just *some* of my needs, but *all* of my needs.

It is the wisdom that comes from my fear of God that helps me to know the difference between what is right and wrong. You can learn to trust God like that, too, son. Believing God and behaving according to His Word will save you much grief and sorrow throughout your life. I have often regretted rash decisions I have made on my own, but I have no regrets about anything I have done that God has led me to do. Even when the journey hasn't been easy, He has made "all things" work together for my good. (See Romans 8:28.)

Proverbs 1:9 (NLT) says, "What you learn from [your parents] will crown you with grace and be a chain of honor around your neck." A crown of grace signifies that wisdom will affect our thinking and enable us to live with dignity and kindness. Our neck helps to keep our head on straight. A chain of honor around the neck suggests that the wisdom we gain will be something of value we will want to carry with us and display proudly, just like a medal.

Voices in Your Head

Keep in mind, son, that whatever you listen to gets into your head. It doesn't stop in your ears; instead, it goes into your mind and becomes part of your thoughts. And whatever gets into your head affects your habits. It is incredible to me that some parents allow their children to watch sinful movies with sexual situations, lying, cussing, fighting and violence, and believe somehow that it is not going to affect these children and their thinking. How could anyone possibly think that children could play an electronic game in which they're blowing people up, cutting off people's heads, stealing cars, breaking out of jail, and raping women, and not realize that such debauchery will get into their heads and affect their habits?

Listening to gangster rap music that degrades women and includes cussing, violence, and stupidity is just setting yourself up for failure. Please don't say, "No, I listen to gangster rap, but I just like the beat. I don't listen to the words." Your brain is not able to dissect what you hear in such a way that only the beat gets in and the words don't come through. Whatever gets into your ears affects your head.

Some people say, "Jeffrey Johnson, do you think you're so holy? Is that why you're so picky about what you see and hear?" No, I don't listen to that stuff because I'm *not* that holy. Whatever gets into my unholy head is going to show up in my unholy lifestyle. That's why I try to get some holiness in my head, instead, so that

44

it will show up in my habits. We've got to make sure that we're getting this issue right with God because everything is coming at us. Peer pressure, ungodly philosophies, advertisements, drugs, pornography, gang bangers—they're all trying to get to us. That's why we've got to learn how to hear God's voice. That's where we will find wisdom. That's where our destiny lies.

Let God Make the Calls

In 2000 Lady Sharon and I went to Baltimore to see the Ravens play early in the football season. We also ended up going to the Super Bowl and watching the Baltimore Ravens play in it as well. We could do this because Kipp Vickers, a former member of our church, was a player with the Baltimore Ravens. This young man played at the University of Miami and got drafted by the Indianapolis Colts. But when the Colts got him, they put him on the practice squad. If somebody got injured, the coach would bring him in to play on the regular team. But when that person got off the injured reserves, Kipp returned to the practice squad. He often went back and forth—back on the team, then back on the practice squad.

Then, suddenly, in 2000, the Baltimore Ravens wanted Kipp on their team. He was so excited because there would be no more practice squads. He would finally be making some decent money and getting a chance to play regularly—all that comes with being a regular player was now his. When he got this new position, he said,

"Pastor, I just want to show my appreciation to those who supported me when my life was up and down." He said that included Lady Sharon and me. So he flew us up to Baltimore, put us up in a hotel, and got us tickets to the game.

This was the year that Tony Banks started the season as a quarterback; but by the end of the year, Trent Gilford took his place and won the Super Bowl with the team. But we were at that early season game. They had the number-one defense in the league and they were really going at it. The crowd was loud—cheering, yelling, and screaming. Sharon happened to notice that after each play, Tony Banks would put his hands over his ears on the helmet. After watching this for a while, she asked, "Jeffrey, what is he doing?"

I replied, "What is who doing?"

"Him—right there. The quarterback. Why does he keep putting his hands over his ears?"

Sure enough, on the next play they advanced the ball, and the crowd was screaming and hollering; but Tony Banks was not giving high fives or participating in the shouting. He had his hands over his ears.

I said to Sharon, "Oh baby, I know what he's doing. He's got a receiver inside his helmet, and his offensive coordinator has a transmitter. Often the coordinators and some of these coaches will sit up in the coach's box high above the field, where they can have a panoramic view and see everything. They can see the line-up and discern the scheme of the opposition's defense that's trying to keep

46

the team from making their goals. But they know that their quarterback—in this game, Tony Banks—has a limited view of what's going on from the field. So, through the transmitter, the coordinator sends in the next play to get Banks and the team to the goal. But Tony Banks has trouble hearing through the receiver in his helmet because even folks who are rooting for him are making too much noise. He has to put his hands over his ears, because I'm sure he's thinking, *I've got to shut out all this outside noise. I need to hear the coordinator send the play in so that I know how to deal with the scheme of the opposition and can get to my goal.*

God is our coach and wisdom is our offensive coordinator. God has put His Spirit inside of us as a receiver to enable us to hear His Word. But our friends and family may be making so much ungodly noise that we can't hear God speak. So we have to shut them out because we need to hear what God has to say. God has a greater perspective than we do. He sees things that we can't see, and He can get us to where we're trying to go.

Envision Yourself as a Learner

Son, let me holla atcha. I love verse 20, which you already read in the opening of this chapter: "Wisdom shouts in the streets." Wisdom isn't just shouting; it's shouting *in the streets*. Wisdom doesn't just shout at God's house; wisdom shouts at *our* house. Wisdom shouts at the crack house. Wisdom shouts at the bars, at the whore house. She doesn't just shout in the pews, she shouts in the public places. I'm so glad there have been times when I've been in a crazy situation and wisdom began to shout, "You're better than this. There's more to you than this. You know you've got no business being in here." That is wisdom shouting in the streets. God is communicating with us.

You also need to see yourself continually learning, son. You can't go through life and not learn anything. Verse 8 says, "My son, listen when your father corrects you. Don't neglect your mother's instruction." What you learn is going to impact the decisions you make and prepare you for all that God has planned for your life. Even if we don't have biological mothers or fathers to give us instruction, God will supply. God has given us spiritual mothers and spiritual fathers to instruct and teach us along the way.

When it comes to learning, son, don't think that you can't learn. Don't let folks trick you into thinking you can't learn. How do I know that you can learn? Because God is never going to tell you to do something you can't do. God will provide for your education so that you can be prepared to follow His calling upon your life. You can handle instruction; you can handle teaching. You need to know that you are capable of learning. You are intelligent. You *can* get a good education. But you have to perceive all this for yourself.

Regrettably, even in this day and age, some folk will look at you as a Black male and immediately think you don't know anything and can't learn anything. You can't let their negative false image define you. You've got to know for yourself who you are and the potential that lies within you. Some men listen to those lies or allow the negative things they feel from others to keep them from following their dreams. They give up, even as young children, and never try to become the people God intended for them to be.

Did you know that the one thing most men in prison have in common is a lack of education? This is true no matter what color they are. The lack of education can lead to incarceration. They don't learn what they need to know in the younger grades, and most of them have dropped out of high school. This is such a common experience that if a boy can't read when he enters third grade, those in the penal system planning for the future prepare to have a bed available when he arrives. In fact, one out of every three black males is going to end up spending time in some kind of prison. But that doesn't have to be you. One of the ways to prevent incarceration is to get an education.

If you've got an education or some specialized kind of training, somebody will pay you for that. People come up to me all the time and ask, "Pastor, can you help me get a job?"

"Well, what can you do?"

"I don't know."

Nobody pays for that. I know a lot of people, but I don't know anybody who will pay someone for "I don't know." You've got to learn something, son.

Be a Victor, Not a Victim

If you are in school and not learning, it may not be the teacher's fault. It could be your fault. If you are taking home Ds and Fs, sometimes it's your fault. If you stay up late at night playing electronic games and are too tired to learn in the classroom, that's your fault. If you show up late for class and try to sneak out early, or even cut class altogether, that's your fault. If you get home from school, grab a basketball, and run to the park instead of doing your homework, that's your fault. If you sit in the back of the classroom when you know you can't see or hear very well, or can't keep your focus on the teacher, that's your fault. (Move to the front so that you can concentrate without being distracted.) If you don't do the work assigned or you don't turn it in on time, that's your fault.

Sometimes it isn't the teacher. You can't always use excuses such as, "She doesn't like me," "The principal doesn't like me," or "They're racist over there." Sometimes it isn't them—it's you. Think about it. If you just come every day to class and show some interest, you'll probably get a D. If you turn in every assignment on time and show that you're trying, you will likely get a C. And if you actually put forth some energy and effort to do your best, you can get an A or B. When you don't put forth effort, don't follow the teacher's instructions, or don't use the brain that God gave you, that's not on the teacher, that's on you.

50

I do understand, however, that there are times when your failure to learn may not be your fault. Sometimes your lack of learning can be on the teacher or on the system. If you walk into class as a Black male and the teacher has no respect for you, sees you as less than who you are, and immediately has low expectations of you, that's your teacher's failure and has nothing to do with you. If you are brighter than your teacher realizes and he or she doesn't know what to do with brilliant children, that's a failure of your teacher, not you.

For instance, if you can finish a forty-five minute test in thirty minutes, your teacher should give you something to do for extra credit, let you start working on your homework, or offer something to occupy your time and attention, rather than sending you to the principal's office for fidgeting for fifteen minutes. If you happen to be a visual learner who grasps information easily when you can see it demonstrated or in print, but your teacher knows only how to teach using a lecture format, that's his or her failure, not yours.

Sometimes when a student is unable to learn, it is an entire system that is at fault. When there are too many students in a class-room so that some of them cannot get the individual attention or help they need, that's a failure of the system. When world history classes begin with White kings and queens in Europe (enabling White children to develop positive self-images), but with Black slaves in America (ignoring the positive images of Black kings and queens in Africa), that's a failure of the system. When primarily White history is taught twelve months a year and Black history is allocated only a couple of hours' class time during February, that's a failure of the system. When a school administers a standardized test acknowledged as culturally biased and then judges a student's intellect as inferior because he or she is not part of the majority culture upon which the test is based, that's a failure of the system. I recognize that sometimes, son, a failure to learn may be the result of a school system that negates you or belittles you, not a personal failure on your part.

But you do not have to be a failure! Hear me well, son. You do not have to become a victim! You need to understand that you can still be a good student even in a bad system. You can be a good student with a bad teacher. If you think your teacher doesn't like you, your principal looks down on you, or the odds at school are stacked against you, use that as fuel to get yourself motivated. Prove to them that they are wrong by showing them. Prove to them that you *can* learn. Prove to them how smart you are. You cannot let a bad system keep you from being good. You've got to see yourself as intelligent and capable of learning. It can happen. It happens across our country thousands upon thousands of times every day. Son, become a part of those who are achieving, not of those who are giving up.

Listening Is Essential

People may say to you, "Why bother? College isn't for everybody." That's true. Prison teaches us that. You don't have to argue that with me. I know that college isn't for everybody. But I'm not talking about everybody; I'm talking about you. You've got to see yourself as the intelligent person God created. You've got to envision yourself learning. You've got to get that education. You've got to use that brain God gave you.

I have told my four sons, "Listen, you ought to be making straight As, but you're coming in here with Bs and Cs. You need to be making straight As. I did, and my genes are in you. You can do it too." One evening, one of my sons came home with some bad grades and I went off in front of some family members who were there. Some of them pulled me aside and said, "Well, Jeffrey, you know everybody isn't going to be like you. Everybody isn't going to get straight As." But I wasn't talking about everybody; I was talking about my four boys. And I'm talking about you too, son. I know college isn't for everybody, but that doesn't mean college isn't for you. Stop letting people convince you of what you cannot do. You can do all things through Christ who gives you strength (Philippians 4:13). You can learn. You can be educated. You can make something of your life. You can do it.

There is one thing, however, that will keep any of us from learning—when we think we already know everything. We refuse to listen to anyone or learn from anyone because we think we know it all. That's why we're admonished in Proverbs 1:8 to listen to instruction. If we don't listen, we can't learn. And when we think we already know everything, then we're not listening. We cannot ignore parents, teachers, mentors, coaches, pastors, employers, and everybody else and somehow think we're going to learn.

No. When we walk into a classroom, we may know *something*, but we may not know what the professor knows. If we are in a seminar or workshop, we don't need to be the one who is doing all of the talking. Why? Because we may not know what the presenter knows. So we need to sit down, be quiet, and listen to what someone else is saying. We cannot learn without listening.

In 1863, Blacks were released from slavery in America, but it was against the law to teach them to read. It was illegal for our fore parents to go to school or to learn how to read, so the majority culture began to call them ignorant: "They're ignorant. They can't read." "They're ignorant. They can't write." The Blacks of that day had a desire for education, but were denied the opportunity. Fast forward to the twenty-first century. Now we have the opportunity, but we don't have the desire. Our fore parents were called ignorant because they were uninformed due to a lack of opportunity. Too many of us are ignorant because we have opportunity, but ignore it. We are ignorant because we ignore those whom God has put in our lives to teach us. We cannot learn if we do not listen.

Don't Give Up

Let me tell you something about my third son, Jalon. He's a very unique person. There's nobody else like Jalon. Yet he had a terrible time in high school. One of the most difficult things for me to do in all of my life was to get my third son through high school. I mean *difficult*. As a child, I lived for several years without a father figure, yet I graduated from high school. I graduated from college. I went to graduate school. I've built plenty of churches. I've planted people in churches. I've even survived cancer. My life has had many challenges. But one of the most difficult things I've ever had to do was to get that boy through high school.

Teachers were calling me, and I was telling Jalon, "Son, I don't want to talk to your teachers unless I'm calling them." But teachers continued to call me. I remember one day sitting around this big old table at school—teachers, educators, a psychologist, a counselor, a principal and *me*. We were there, I was told, because this boy was terrorizing his teachers. I made it clear to Jalon: "Son, stop terrorizing your teachers."

At that point I thought, *Maybe he's got a learning disability.* So I arranged to have all sorts of tests given to Jalon. This boy scored off the charts! In addition, he was coming home and reading really thick books such as *Moby Dick, Sherlock Holmes, A Tale of Two Cities,* and others most of us wouldn't be interested in. These weren't reading assignments for the class. These were just books he wanted to read on his own. Yet in class he continued to just scrape by. I often asked Jalon, "Son, why are you doing this? You've proven that you can handle it. You can do the work." But I could never get a good answer from him.

It took everything I had to get this boy through high school—so much so, that I had already planned to take the money I had set aside for his college education to buy a house in Florida instead. I told Jalon, "You don't want to go to college? Fine. I'll get a vacation home in Florida."

But after he got out of high school, there was a college that let this boy in! I'm not kidding. *Somebody let this boy in school.* I was shocked. And, on top of that, he has made all As and Bs. He is even on course to graduate a year and a half early. He's called me saying, "I don't know if I'm going to go to graduate school in New York or in Chicago . . . ." It really was only when I saw Jalon succeed in college that I realized he was not at fault for his failure to succeed in high school. He was not being challenged there at the level of his potential. He grew bored with the busy work he was assigned and eventually it affected his attitude and behavior.

Sometimes the failure may not be your fault, son. But Jalon only made it through to the next level because he had parents who recognized how important it was for him to get that diploma so that he could move on to the next opportunity. He had parents who kept pushing him, kept helping him, and kept expecting more from him.

Son, whether or not you have a father or a mother who pushes you to keep moving on in school, *you* have to understand what is going on. *You* have to wake up and get what you need to get so that you can go on to the next level. I don't care what grade you are in at school or even if you have already dropped out and wasted some

56

time along the way—you can still turn it around! You can still do what you need to do to get that high school diploma. Then you can go to college to get a degree, or attend technical school to gain your specialized training, so that you can fulfill the potential God placed in you when He created you. He didn't create you to be ignorant. He created you with the capacity to learn. The fact that you are reading this book proves that. If you can read and understand this book, you have the potential to do great things with your life.

If I Only Had a Brain

My awesome friend Dr. Kevin Cosby pastors St. Stephens Church in Louisville, Kentucky and Jeffersonville, Indiana, (one church in two states), and he is the president of Simmons College. In addressing a group of people, he said, "Listen. You've got to get your brain together."

Now, that is important because some foolish boys keep thinking that people are afraid of them. Nobody is afraid of them. They walk around with their behinds showing out of their pants. Their hair looks crazy. They don't know how to dress themselves. They dropped out of school. And they are dealing drugs on a street corner. They've never even been out of their own neighborhood, and yet they arrogantly say, "This block is mine." With nothing more than their empty boasting, they somehow think that folks are afraid of them. Nobody is afraid of that.

A story in the New Testament tells about a man filled with evil spirits. He would cut himself, break chains, run up into the mountains, come back down, and sleep in the cemetery. He was comfortable hanging out with dead people and staying in a dead environment. He wouldn't comb his hair and would often take his clothes off in inappropriate places. This man was crazy. Nobody was afraid of him. But one day he met Jesus. After his encounter with Jesus, Luke 8:35 says he was clothed, in his right mind, sitting at the feet of Jesus. And *then*, the people were afraid.

Nobody is afraid when a man is walking around butt naked in the wrong places, hurting himself, never leaving his neighborhood, and hanging out in dead places. People today are not afraid of the man at the crack house. But they are afraid of President Barack Obama at the White House. They know that he's got his stuff together. When he steps out, he knows how to walk and knows how to talk. People know that his influence is real. It is backed by intelligence, education, experience, and a position to which others elected him, not a title he is trying to get simply by boasting.

In talking to the group about getting their brain together, Dr. Cosby told them, "Nobody is going to take you seriously until you've got your brain straight." He brought up the scarecrow in *The Wizard of Oz* as an illustration. Nobody takes him seriously—not even the crows. As a scarecrow, he's supposed to be scaring the crows away, but they're flying all around him, sitting on him, picking at him, and even messing on him. He finally realizes why nobody takes him seriously. He wistfully tells Dorothy when she comes by, "If I only had a brain . . ." Recognizing his need for a brain, the scarecrow decides to go to the Emerald City and ask the wizard for one. So here's what he does. He gets off the stick and gets on the yellow brick road to go and get his brain.

On the journey to get his brain, it finally dawns on the scarecrow that he has something to offer after all. He begins getting his thoughts together. Remember that the scarecrow is the one who comes up with all the ideas on the road to the Emerald City. He's the one who thinks of ways to deal with the wicked witch and the flying monkeys, as well as what to do with the witch's broom. Because he gets off the stick and gets on the right road, he discovers that he has something going on in his head after all. When he returns to the Emerald City after the death of the witch, the wizard even appoints him to be the mayor!

I'm trying to tell you, son, that if you are in the same situation as the scarecrow, as soon as you get off the stick—or the pipe, or whatever it is you're on—and get on the right road, you will learn that you've got something to offer. You've got to start seeking life. Life is about choices. Proverbs 1:10-14 (NLT) says,

> My child, if sinners entice you, turn your back on them! They may say, "Come and join us. Let's hide and kill someone! Just for fun, let's ambush the innocent! Let's swallow them alive, like the grave;

let's swallow them whole, like those who go down to
the pit of death. Think of the great things we'll get!
We'll fill our houses with all the stuff we take. Come,
throw in your lot with us; we'll all share the loot."

It sounds like gang activity, doesn't it? That's just what it is. It's organized crime in the street. Solomon is saying in this verse that when sinners entice you to hook up with them to steal, kill people, and work together to do evil, just turn your back on them. Just don't do it. Walk away from them instead. Just say no. In the early '80s, when drugs were on the rise in America, we had a drug czar who waged a war against drugs, and a number of federal offices were dealing with this issue. Yet First Lady Nancy Reagan had the best idea of all about how to deal with drugs: "Just say no."

Just Say No!

Dr. James Dobson says that teenagers who are fifteen and sixteen years old don't have the psychological capacity to evaluate consequences. We say, "Don't do it because this or that will happen to you." But they don't have the psychological capacity to be able to assess a situation like that. They don't understand that if they steal, they could: go to juvenile center, have a strike against them, be expelled from school, impact their family in a negative way, or any of that. They don't have the capacity to understand their own vulnerability. They don't consider that if they have sex, they might get a sexually transmitted disease or an unwanted pregnancy, which would mess their lives up permanently. They don't have the psychological capacity to understand what killing someone would do to the victim's family, to the community, and to our society.

But even if teens don't have the psychological competence to understand all the consequences for their actions, we all have the capacity to discern right from wrong. We may not have the ability to deal with the consequences, but we do have the ability to make the right choices. God has given us His wisdom and if something doesn't line up with what God's Word says, then we know we don't need to be doing it.

Just say no to drugs, no to alcohol, no to promiscuity, no to pornography, no to gang violence, and no to dealing drugs. All you've got to do is just say no! In Deuteronomy 30:19 Moses says, "I have set before you life and death, blessings and curses. Now choose life so that you and your children may live." That's what it's all about, son. You've got a choice to make. There are only two options—life or death. It's Jesus or Satan, heaven or hell. You may not have the capacity to deal with consequences, but you know right from wrong. And if you do what is right, you can trust God to handle the consequences.

Why would at-risk boys get caught up in gang violence? Why wouldn't they choose God over gangs, work over stealing, victory over violence, liberty over bondage, liberation over incarceration, peace over confusion, love over hate, heaven over hell, salvation over death, and loving somebody to life over beating somebody to death? Why wouldn't they do that? Why would they want to join a gang and get caught up in the violence that goes with it?

The experts say it's about belonging, respect, money, and protection. When our at-risk boys are enticed to join a gang, they go ahead and do it, thinking, *I need to be connected to someone. I didn't get that feeling of belonging in my family, so I need to find it somewhere else. Nobody respects me or honors me. Even my teachers look down on me, and my community doesn't even acknowledge my existence. Even those who wrote the Constitution think I'm less than human. I need to find somewhere that I can get some respect. I need to be protected. I need somebody to have my back. I need some money. I'm tired of being poor. I need to eat and I need to get clothes, so this is the way I'm going to do it.*

But son, I'm trying to tell you that you don't have to go that direction. You don't have to turn your life into the abyss of gangs and violence, drug addiction, ignorance and stupidity, and lack of education. There are others just as vulnerable who have the same sort of family as you do. They don't get respect and often find themselves in dire financial need, but they don't choose gangs. They get a sense of belonging by being in a club, on a sports team, or in a fraternity.

Personally, I get family connections and a sense of belonging in the church. That's why we call each other brothers and sisters — we're family. I get my protection from my relationship with God. I don't have to worry about money. God knows how to pay bills. God knows how to find tuition money. God knows how to start businesses. I'm not sweating that. I've got all I need in God.

Verse 18 says that when sinners get caught up in violence, robbery, and abuse, they think they are setting a trap for other folks, but they're actually setting a trap for themselves. In other words, you reap what you sow. Life has a boomerang effect. What you throw out comes back at you. You are really hurting yourself when you treat others badly.

Talk Truth to Yourself

The movie *Looper*, was set in the year 2044. . The character Joe, played by Bruce Willis, gets into a time machine and goes back thirty years to confront his previous self, the man he used to be, played by Joseph Gordon-Levitt. Everything this past Joe is doing is affecting the future Joe. Since the future Joe already knows what's going to happen and knows the ramifications of his actions, he goes back to the past to have a talk with himself. He first tells his younger self about a specific situation and advises him, "When you find yourself in this situation, run as far away as you can." So when the situation comes up, the middle-aged Joe goes by to see if the young Joe took his advice and ran away. While sitting in a café, the older Joe says to the younger one, "You idiot. Didn't I tell you to run? Everything you're doing now is affecting you in the future."

As I watched that movie, I was thinking to myself, *I wish I had a time machine*. I want to go back and tell the twenty-year-old Jeffrey Johnson, "When you see this certain situation, run!" "When you see this person coming, run!" "When you see this type of environment, run!" "When this woman walks up to you, RUN!!!" I want to go back and say to the twenty-year-old Jeffrey Johnson, "You idiot! Everything you are doing now will affect you later. You are hurting yourself."

You Have a Savior

Then, here's what the older Joe from the future told his younger self in *Looper*: "You know what? As messed up as you are, you're going to meet somebody, and that person is going to save your life."

"What's the person's name?"

"Don't worry about what the name is. Worry about why. Why would anyone save you? You are nothing but a liar, a cheater, a killer, a murderer, a drug addict, and an alcoholic. Why would someone save you? But you are saved anyway."

Here's what I want to tell you, son. You may have made bad choices, and your past has messed you up. But there is Somebody who will save your life. The question you need to ask yourself is, *Why would anyone save someone like me? I've lied, cheated, gotten high, stolen, murdered, assaulted, and have had children out of wedlock whom I haven't even acknowledged. I've done so many bad things. Why would anyone save me?* I can tell you the name of the One who will save you. His name is Jesus. And the reason He will save you is because He loves you.

No matter where you are, He will save you. Whether you are reading this book in the comfort of your own home, in the confines of a prison, or sitting in a homeless shelter—wherever you are—Jesus is there with you. Despite all of your mistakes, He loves you. No matter what you have done, the blood of Jesus Christ can cleanse you from all of your sin and give you a fresh start. Ask His forgiveness and commit your life to Him, and you will find yourself headed in an entirely different direction. God can do amazing things in the life of the individual who belongs to Him.

An Example to Consider: David

Please take out your Bible and read 2 Samuel 11 – 12 and Psalm 51.

David was anointed by God at an early age to become king over Israel. Eventually, he was appointed by God to the place He had designed for him. You would think that David had everything any man would want—a relationship with God, wealth, power, respect, family, friends, and anything money could buy. Yet David wasn't satisfied. When he saw Bathsheba, he felt he had to have her. He committed adultery with her and then had her husband killed in an attempt to cover up the affair. David would not have believed that he was capable of adultery and murder, but once he sought to please himself rather than God, his downward spiral was rapid.

After his friend Nathan confronted him, David realized he could no longer hide his sin. Sorrowful and ashamed, he confessed his sin before God. It was in that moment that forgiveness and restoration came to him. As long as he was trying to cover his sin, there was a big separation between him and God. Guilt was his constant companion. But 1 John 1:9 says, "If we confess our sins, he is faithful and just and will forgive us our sins and purify us from all unrighteousness." As soon as David confessed his sin, God was faithful to forgive his sins and to cleanse him from all his unrighteousness.

Son, this will hold true for you too. You undoubtedly have done things, as we all have, that you wish you hadn't done—things that felt good to you at the time, but left you feeling guilty and ashamed. You don't need to continue to feel that way. You don't have to continue to live at a distance from God. God still loves you. God wants to be close to you. God is just waiting to forgive your sins. All you need to do is ask. Jesus already died and shed His blood on the cross so that your sins can be forgiven and you can walk together with your heavenly Father. If you are ready, just pray this prayer from your heart:

Dear God,

I am ashamed to even come to You because of what I've done. I know that You are holy, and I am so unholy. But I long to be in a relationship with You. I don't want to feel guilty anymore. I don't want to be far away from You. Please forgive me of my sins. Even as You did for David, please cleanse me of all unrighteousness. Please take my life, and help me to live to please You and not myself. Thank You, Jesus, for dying for me so that I might live. Thank You, God, for loving me. Thank You for letting me know that there is still hope for me. I love You, God, and I am so thankful for Your forgiveness. Amen.

CHAPTER 2

God's Gotcha

He grants a treasure of common sense to the honest.

He is a shield to those who walk with integrity.

He guards the paths of the just

and protects those who are faithful to him.

Proverbs 2:7-8, NLT

Life Ain't Easy

One of my favorite poems is "Mother to Son," by Langston Hughes. In the poem, a mother encourages her son never to give up. She tells him that, just as she kept going despite all the difficulties and challenges in life she faced, he needs to follow her example and keep climbing too. Langston Hughes was just twenty years old when he wrote that poem. Even though he was young, he had already learned that life can be difficult.

Life can go bad on us. Hard times and harassments can take place in our lives. It doesn't matter how holy we think we are either. Everybody's going to go through something. God has had one Son who knew no sin, but He has not had any sons who have known no suffering.

Jesus Christ was tempted like we are, but He never sinned. Yet He did know suffering. He knew what it was to be bullied. He knew what it was to be taunted and teased. He knew what it was for people close to Him to betray and forsake Him. He knew what it was to be whipped and beaten, for His hands to have nails pounded through them, and for His feet to have spikes holding Him to a cross.

But in the midst of all of that, God had not forsaken Him. God had not walked out on Him. Hebrews 2:9 explains that Jesus died in our place for the sins we have committed, but because He suffered that death, He was "crowned with glory and honor." The full verse reads, "But we do see Jesus, who was made lower than the angels for a little while, now crowned with glory and honor because he suffered death, so that by the grace of God he might taste death for everyone."

Some people think that when they run into pitfalls, predicaments, and painful situations, God has forsaken them. No, God's gotcha. It's just that sometimes He has to take you *through* something to get you *to* something. As Psalm 23:4-5 says: "Even though I walk through the darkest valley, I will fear no evil, for you are with me; your rod and your staff, they comfort me. You prepare a table before me in the presence of my enemies.

You anoint my head with oil; my cup overflows." Notice that the anointing is on the other side of the dark valley. The overflowing cup—the place of abundance—is on the other side of the dark valley. The table prepared for me in the presence of my enemies is on the other side of the dark valley.

Dark valleys may *seem* scary, but we can recognize as the psalmist did in Psalm 23:4: "I will fear no evil, for you are with me; your rod and your staff, they comfort me." We do not walk alone when we go through the dark valleys. But we do have to walk through them because so much of what we need and so much of what we want are on the other side. By taking us through the dark valleys, God is setting us up for what He has for us. When we believe that Jesus died on the cross and that God raised Him from the dead, and accept this Jesus into our lives for forgiveness of sin, God has promised *never* to leave us, never to forsake us.

God Is Our Shield

Remember that Proverbs 2:7 (NLT) says, "He is a shield to those who walk with integrity." God protects us along our journey, even when that journey takes us through the dark valleys. Solomon, who wrote these words, was addressing some of the young men who would be the future leaders of Israel. He was telling them what they needed in order to be leaders. One of the things they needed was a shield. In those days, as soldiers went into battle, they had their swords in one hand, and their shields in the other. The sword provided their offense; the shield provided their defense. Solomon was telling them in this verse that God is the shield that protects them.

But sometimes we may wonder, *If God is shielding and protecting me, then why is all this stuff going on in my life?* The young men to whom Solomon spoke knew that in order for their shield to be effective, they had to keep it close to them. If the shield was held out to the side, allowed to fall to the ground, or kept at a distance, there was too much space left open for the enemy to attack. Sadly, we sometimes have a tendency to distance ourselves from our Shield. How can we benefit from God being our shield when we don't maintain closeness to God? We need to stay close to Him, to have the intimacy of relationship that He desires to have with us. He wants to protect us, but how can He do this if we are running off by ourselves or keeping Him at a distance? We have to stay close to the Shield.

In those days, shields were very big. They were so big, in fact, that when a soldier was under attack, he could put his whole body behind his shield. By likening God to a shield, Solomon is trying to tell us that our God is so big, we can put our whole selves behind Him. We can think holistically when it comes to God. He can protect our mentality, our emotions, our physical health, our spirits—all of our being. God can safely hold our families, the ministries in which we are engaged, our educational opportunities, and the companies we own. We can take everything that we are and everything that we have, and line it all up behind the Lord; and He can protect us, along with everything that we place in His care.

Protection Is Not Always Prevention

One of the ways God sometimes protects us is by not letting certain things happen in our lives. As we reflect upon our past, we know there are some things that *would* have happened to us, *could* have happened to us, and even *should* have happened to us, yet they didn't happen to us. Why? God prevented them from happening because He is our shield. Things aren't kept from happening to us because we're so intelligent, or we're so good, or we're so clever, but because God is our shield. Even when we haven't been aware that something bad was creeping up on us, God saw it and prevented it from harming us.

But wait a minute. You may be saying, "But God doesn't always protect me. There are some really bad things that have happened to me—some trials that I had to face, some tragedies that I had to endure, some difficulties that I had to overcome." Yes, that's true. God doesn't always *prevent* things from happening to us. Sometimes, He *permits* certain things to happen. As Christians we don't lead a charmed life that exempts us from pain and suffering. When we come to Christ and give our lives to Him, it isn't because He is going to let us live a life of luxury and ease until we someday go to heaven. If we believe that, we are going to be totally disillusioned when tough times come our way. We need only to read the Bible to realize that following God is not an easy road.

What we need to remember, however, is that God can take the trials, the tragedies, and the difficulties and use them for good in our lives. No, they aren't good in themselves. They offend our sense of justice. They confuse us. And they hurt—sometimes so deeply that we wonder if we will ever be whole again. But Romans 8:28 is true: "And we know that in *all things* God works for the good of those who love him, who have been called according to his purpose" (italics mine). God knows what to let in and what to keep out. God knows what to let touch us and what to keep away from us. God knows what to send us through and what to lead us around. When God allows something to happen in our lives, we can be sure that He will use it for a purpose in our lives. He will never allow His children to suffer in vain. There is always a reason, always some greater good that will come from it.

Sometimes God allows negative circumstances to redirect our lives so that we don't miss the plans and purposes He has for us. Sometimes God allows us to go through things in order to strengthen us. Think about it. When you are trying to become stronger and physically fit, you go to the gym and work out. You pick up something heavy to build your muscles. But you don't pick it up just one time. You do it day by day, adding more weight as you go along, because you know lifting that weight is making you stronger.

Similarly, God knows that you need to build your strength for the days ahead. He knows what is in store for you. He knows that to be a good husband, father, teacher, scientist, doctor, pastor, senator—or whatever it is He has planned for your life—you will need spiritual strength. Right now, when He looks at you, He sees a spiritual weakling. So God says, "I need to let my son carry some heavier weight so that he can grow stronger. I know the man that he is going to become, so I need to allow some things in his life that will strengthen him, give him wisdom, and teach him resilience." God doesn't allow hard times to come to hurt us, but to help us. He doesn't allow difficulties to come to defeat us, but to strengthen us.

Discipline Avoids Destruction

Sometimes God allows things to happen in our lives because He is seeking to discipline us, or to "correct" us. If we are God's sons, and we are moving in the wrong direction and doing the wrong things, God will say, "Hold it. I love you too much to let you keep going in the wrong direction. I have to correct you so you won't get hurt." So, how does God correct us? God will often use what other people do against us in order to correct us.

Just look at the children of Israel. They sinned against God, were disobedient to Him, and got caught up in idolatry. God loved them too much to let them continue down a path of permanent destruction. So God allowed Nebuchadnezzar and the Babylonian army to come and deal with the Israelites until they eventually returned to Him and again followed His ways.

This is not unlike the behavior of the father in the parable of the prodigal son. When the son demanded to have his inheritance immediately, when he refused the safety of his father's house, and arrogantly set out on his own, the father did not lock him in his room and forbid him to do what was in his heart to do. The father knew that his son would never change if he protected him from himself, so he let him go his own way and allowed the world to teach him some lessons. The world did not love the young man as his father did. The world used him, abused him, and left him hungry and destitute; he even had to eat from a trough with pigs. But this painful lesson taught the young man that he was not as smart as he thought he was. It taught him that he needed his father and his father's guidance. It taught him that there was love and safety in his father's home, and it softened his heart so that he could return and repent.

God, the heavenly Father, chastens those He loves. Hebrews 12:7-8 admonishes us, "Endure hardship as discipline; God is treating you as his children. For what children are not disciplined by their father? If you are not disciplined—and everyone undergoes discipline—then you are not legitimate, not true sons and daughters at all." God disciplines those He loves. He's saying, "Here's what I'm going to do. I'm going to allow you to have painful consequences for your disobedience so that I can teach you to obey Me."

Similarly, as an earthly father I had to teach my own sons to obey me and their mother for their own good by letting them experience some painful consequences for their disobedience. For instance, I let them play freely in our yard. They could play any game or sport they wanted to in the yard—dodge ball, kickball, baseball, football, whatever they wanted. But I instructed them clearly, "Do not go in the street. Don't even go near the street. Even if the ball goes into the street, you come into the house and get me, but you do not go in the street." After I had warned them, if I saw my sons go anywhere *near* the street, I would discipline them. I had to do that because I love them. Proverbs 13:24 says, "Whoever spares the rod hates their children, but the one who loves their children is careful to discipline them." I love my children too much to allow them to be disobedient without any consequences.

Now, understand clearly that discipline without love is abuse. Whatever the form of discipline, if there is no love in it, it's abuse. I know some people don't believe in spanking, but I believe that administering a little controlled pain to our children in the moment can help them avoid extreme pain later on. I was willing to allow my children to experience a little pain for disobeying me about going into the street so that they would avoid the extreme pain, and possible death, from being hit by a car. They didn't really recognize their vulnerability as a child who could be hit by a car, but they could understand that if Daddy says don't go into the street, he means it. By learning to avoid painful consequences through their obedience to me, they avoided severe consequences that they didn't fully realize existed.

Discipline through Denial

Not all discipline comes through physical pain. When I was ten years old, I *wanted* my mother to spank me when I was disobedient instead of using some other form of discipline. A spanking took only a few seconds. I used to silently wish, *Don't take me off the basketball team! Don't make me stop playing football! Don't tell me to stay in the house! Those forms of discipline last too long and hurt too much. Just give me my few seconds of physical pain. I'll take it like a ten-year-old man and then go on with my life.* But, sometimes, I needed to experience a different sort of discipline—one that would last longer and affect me more deeply.

Every now and then, our Father God may keep us from enjoying certain privileges as a form of discipline. There may be something you want to do, but God says, "I'm not going to let that happen because I need to teach you obedience." There are places you've wanted to go, but God says, "No, I need for you to understand what is happening here. You need to recognize that you are drifting away and you need to come back."

God knows us so well and loves us so much that He knows what form of discipline will be most effective in correcting us. When my sons disobeyed me, I didn't simply send them to their room to discipline them. That would have been like sending them to Disneyland. With all the toys and games I had bought them, they could have stayed there, happy and content, for days. If I sent them to their room, I had to first remove some of the things I had given them so that they would have time to think and learn the lesson I needed to teach them. At times that's how God disciplines us. He essentially says, "I will remove certain privileges and certain possessions out of your life because I love you too much for you to continue moving in the wrong direction. I have to discipline you to get you back on track." God's discipline does not mean He is not protecting us. On the contrary, it means He *is* protecting us.

Obedience Means Now

God also wants us to learn to obey Him immediately. There are times we can be putting our own lives in danger if we do not obey Him at once. This holds true in other realms as well. That's why I never told my children more than once to do something. You would never hear me telling one of my sons, "This is the third time I've told you . . . ." No. They knew that when I told them to do something once, I expected them to do it immediately.

Why did I teach them that? Once they learned that from me, their teacher wouldn't have to tell them more than once to sit down. Once they learned it from me, a police officer would never have to tell them more than once to stop running. A teacher might not tell them more than once to sit down; instead, he or she might send them to the principal's office, where the consequences could be severe. I would never expect my sons to be in a situation in which they would be running from something, but a police officer might not tell them more than once to stop running. The consequences of their failure to obey him could be extreme. So I'm going to discipline them now so that they will not be in a position later on that could result in severe outcomes.

God's discipline doesn't mean He doesn't love us. He *is* protecting us. He *is* our shield. But He takes us through this discipline and development so that we can be what He wants us to be. After telling us in verse 7 that God is a shield to us, Proverbs 2:8-12 says,

> For he guards the course of the just and protects the way of his faithful ones. Then you will understand what is right and just and fair—every good path. For wisdom will enter your heart, and knowledge will be pleasant to your soul. Discretion will protect you, and understanding will guard you. Wisdom will save you from the ways of wicked men, from men whose words are perverse.

Wisdom from the Word

How does God protect us? By giving us wisdom through His Word and then helping us to discern right from wrong. So now, the wise choices watch over us. His Word gives us principles and parameters to live by. If we follow them, then we have the protection of God. But if we decide we're not going to live by these principles, then we're living outside the protective hand of God. Get this: the blessings are within the boundaries.

We already know some of the ethics God has put in His Word that tell us how to live. In Luke 10:27 Jesus quoted the Torah, "'Love the Lord your God with all your heart and with all your soul and with all your strength and with all your mind,' and, 'Love your neighbor as yourself'" (Deuteronomy 6:5; Leviticus 19:18). We know the Ten Commandments: "You shall have no other gods before me. You shall not make for yourself an image . . . . You shall not misuse the name of the Lord . . . . Remember the Sabbath day by keeping it holy . . . . Honor your father and your mother . . . . You shall not murder. You shall not commit adultery. You shall not steal. You shall not give false testimony against your neighbor. You shall not covet." (See Exodus 20:3-17.)

These and other portions of Scripture let us know the parameters set by God. But when we decide that we are not going to operate within these principles, we can't get angry at God if trauma comes into our lives as a result. If there is a sign that says, "Beware of

relate to you properly or won't have the proper expectations of you. It doesn't mean you won't run into some bad school systems. It doesn't mean that you won't run into a racist or find yourself in a prejudiced situation. It doesn't mean that you won't run into injustice, even in a justice system. It doesn't mean that you won't run into social injustice in our society. What it does mean is that even though you're attacked, those attacking you won't get an advantage over you because God is protecting you with His wisdom and His Word.

Let me share with you a very sad experience, but one that illustrates this point. In North Fort Myers, Florida, a woman's mind snapped. Something went terribly wrong in this woman's head. She took a gun, and shot and killed her two-year-old child. This was her own son, just two years old. Then she took the gun, jumped in her car, and drove down to a storefront church, where her sixteen-year-old son was inside, worshiping God. He had no idea that his mother was preparing to kill him in a drive-by shooting. The same gun that was used against his little brother was being used against him as well. As he came out of the church, his mother raised that weapon, shot it, and the bullet hit its mark. But the boy didn't die; he didn't even get injured. You may wonder how that was possible, but think about it. He had been in the church worshiping.

Songwriter Jonathan Nelson has said, "My praise is my weapon." There is something about praising and glorifying God that brings a protective measure to your life. In Psalm 42:4, the psalmist wrote, "These things I remember as I pour out my soul: how I used to go to the house of God *under the protection of the Mighty One* with shouts of joy and praise among the festive throng" (italics mine).

But not only had this boy been in church praising God, when he came out, a reporter noted that he was wearing an overcoat and carrying a big Bible in his hand. When his mother fired the gun, the bullet hit the Bible first. By the time it went through the Bible and then his overcoat (those things that had the boy covered), the bullet could not prosper. It could not harm him. There is a spiritual principle illustrated in this. If you have been studying and living by God's Word, and are covered by the blood of Jesus, when enemies come against you, no weapon that is formed against you shall be able to prosper. The Word of God and blood of Jesus will protect you.

Deliver Us from Evil People

God is a shield, and He will act as a shield to protect you. Proverbs 2:12-15 (NLT) says, "Wisdom will save you from evil people, from those whose words are twisted. These men turn from the right way to walk down dark paths. They take pleasure in doing wrong, and they enjoy the twisted ways of evil. Their actions are crooked, and their ways are wrong." God is basically saying, "I'm going to save you from those people." We need to be saved from people who want to harm us.

God has already saved us from sin. As Romans 3:23 says, "For all have sinned and fall short of the glory of God." None of us has lived a sinless life. But Jesus died on the cross to pay the penalty for our sin. Romans 6:23 tells us: "For the wages of sin is death, but the gift of God is eternal life in Christ Jesus our Lord."

We are saved from sin because we have put our faith in Jesus, but we continually need to be saved from people who would turn us away from Him. A lot of us are being hindered in our walk with God and our desire to live meaningful lives because of other people. When we run with wayward folks who use wicked words, deviate from the ways of God, and operate in darkness, it won't be long before we are following them instead of God. Such people offer us no revelation about who God is, no enlightenment about the Word of God, and no inspiration to follow Him, so why are we running with them? God says, "I'm going to save you from such people." And we need that.

No Man Is an Island

But God doesn't intend to remove *all* people from our lives. We need others in our lives. There are people whom God can use to help us to grow closer to Him and to live lives of purpose. We should never try to be an island all to ourselves. God never intended us to live in isolation. Even in the very beginning, God gave Adam someone with whom to share his life. It was also God's idea for us to be born into families.

God even refers to the church as the body of Christ, of which we are each members. Within the body, God has given each believer a spiritual gift. No one person has every gift, but every believer has at least one gift. These spiritual gifts are meant to be used for the edifying and building up of the body of Christ. So, when you use the gift you have been given, it edifies and builds up others. God uses His people to care for one another.

When you think about your own history, you will recognize that there has been someone along the way who has made a positive difference in your life. There was some teacher, minister, coach, mentor, parent, friend—somebody—whom God has used to edify and build you up. God saves us from the people who tear us down, but He puts us in relationships with those who will build us up.

Right Motive, Wrong People

We need other people, but we need to choose our close friends wisely. If you ask the positive adult figures in your life what one of their biggest mistakes they've ever made was, I can guarantee you at least one of them will reply, "I connected with the wrong person." Whether it's hanging out with the wrong person, dating the wrong person, going into business with the wrong person, or even marrying the wrong person, this can be one of the most traumatic and damaging experiences in life. The wrong people can mess us up.

Kirk Franklin learned that lesson. We know that Kirk is a great gospel artist and song writer. While trying to reach young people through gospel music, he added a hip-hop flavor to get their attention. On one of his CDs, he did a collaborative piece with Mary J. Blige and R. Kelly. They took Bill Withers' song, "Lean on Me," and adapted it by adding a little gospel and hip-hop. It was a good experience initially, but not long after that, R. Kelly got a lot of negative notoriety that detracted from the message Kirk Franklin wanted to promote. Because of his association with R. Kelly, Kirk took a lot of flak from his critics. Recognizing that the cause of Christ was being compromised, Kirk made up his mind right then and there that he would only work in the future with Spirit-filled Christians.

It wasn't enough for Kirk to work with people who were wealthy and famous and could attract a crowd. He realized that he is known by the company he keeps and he didn't want the young people he was influencing to be affected in a negative way. He was singing the song, "Lean on Me," but could the young people listening to that song lean on Bill Withers, R. Kelly, or Mary J. Blige? They needed to know that the One they ultimately need to lean on and trust is God Himself. When we place our trust in Him, He will save us from the people who would drag us down.

Use the Sense You're Given

How is God going to save us from evil people? Proverbs 2:12 says, "*Wisdom* will save you from the ways of wicked men, from men whose words are perverse," and verse 6 says, "For the Lord gives wisdom." God is essentially saying, "Son, I'm going to give you enough sense that you won't mess around with folks who use wicked words. I'm going to give you enough sense for you to determine who you should be with and shouldn't be with." God gives us wisdom and good sense, but it's up to us to apply that to our lives.

I like listening to all kinds of music—classical, gospel, the blues, etc. But here's the thing: I've got enough sense not to pay singers to cuss me out. I'm not buying their CD or paying to download their music so that they can call me the n-word or fill my mind with words a Christian should never be thinking. I've got enough sense from God to be delivered from these wicked words. I'm not going to invite such things into my life.

My wife and I both enjoy *some* things; however, there are other things I like that Sharon can't stand. Likewise, she enjoys doing some things that I can't stand. But we don't try to make each other do what we know the other one hates to do. Instead, we've decided, "Let's find something to do that we both enjoy and appreciate. Then we can both have a good time together."

One of those things we've discovered we both enjoy is comedy. But some comedians use words in their routines that wouldn't be acceptable in other venues. So God said to me, "Jeffrey Johnson, I'm going to give you enough sense to save you from wicked words." That means I have enough sense not to pay forty dollars to have somebody cuss at me. I'm not going to pay anyone to call me the n-word. I'm not going to support someone who demeans or disrespects women. And I'm definitely not going to sit and listen while someone uses the name of my God in vain. I've got enough God-given sense that I will not put myself in a position to listen to such wickedness.

Who Does God Say You Are?

One thing I've learned is that once I have firmly placed God's Word in my mind, it helps me to overcome wickedness. We can't always stop people from taunting or bullying us with words, but if we have God's Word inside of us, we can overcome them with verses that come to our remembrance. For example, 1 John 3:1-2 says, "See what great love the Father has lavished on us, that we should be called children of God! And that is what we are! The reason the world does not know us is that it does not know Him. Dear friends, now we are children of God." What does it matter what others call us if we know that God calls us His children? When we know who we are because of what God has told us, nothing someone else says holds any weight. My son, you are a child of God, a son of the King. Don't ever forget that.

My youngest son's name is Josiah, but I usually call him "K.J." Some people wonder why I do that. I call him K.J. because he was named after the eight-year-old boy in the Bible who became king of Israel. His name is really Josiah, but the "K" stands for "King." For fifteen years, K.J. has heard me call him "King." By simply hearing me call him "K.J.," my son has heard me confer upon him authority, nobility, prosperity, and royalty. If someone else comes along and calls him by a derogatory name, he won't need to be bothered by it because he heard what his father has called him all these years.

When we read God's Word, we learn what He thinks about us. For instance, in Psalm 139:14, we learn that we are "fearfully and wonderfully made." When someone calls us a name, we don't have to be troubled because we know who we are.

It's Ludicrous!

Sometimes it isn't a bully, a gangster rapper, or a racist who calls us names. Sometimes we say these wicked words ourselves. You have probably known someone personally who uses the n-word like it's a badge of honor.

I remember a few years ago when Rev. Al Sharpton called me and said, "We need for you to do something in Indy. We're going to go to radio stations all over the country and ask them to stop playing music that has the n-word in it. Our children are the ones listening to that music, and we want the stations to stop playing it. We are the ones who support the sponsors that keep them on the air, so we need to let them know we don't like it and want it to stop." So I went to Radio One in downtown Indy, one of the most popular radio stations in the city. Some other local pastors and people from our congregations gathered at the station to let them know we were serious about this issue. When we talked with the station's leaders, they agreed with us and said they would stop playing that sort of music.

The very next week, I was at an inner-city car wash where I know they do a good job. There were some brothers at the car wash that day not working there, but just hanging out. As they talked, Rev. Al Sharpton's name came up, and these brothers started criticizing him. I couldn't believe it. They were saying, "How dare he get on us for using the n-word in our music and when we rap?" Then they brought up the First Amendment. They said, "Doesn't Al Sharpton know we've got freedom of speech and expression?" I was thinking, *You've got freedom of speech, but you want to use that freedom to call yourself the n-word?*

It's like being a rapper who doesn't want to use his real name, but the best alternative he could come up with is "Ludicrous." It *is* ludicrous! Can't we call ourselves by names worthy of who we are? If we want to build our self-esteem, we've got to begin saying what God says about us.

Avoid the Fleas

Son, I also want you to know that God delivers us not only from wicked words, but also from waywardness. There are people who deviate from the ways of God, delighting in wrongdoing and walking in ways of darkness. God says to us, "I've given you too much sense to hang around that kind of people." So, we've got to be careful whom we associate with because people can mess us up.

You may say, "I know my friends do a lot of stuff that I shouldn't do. But they're my friends. I'm just hanging out with them. I don't do what they do." But I can tell you that if the police come to arrest a group that's hanging around and getting into trouble, they aren't going to leave you out because you say that you don't do what they do. You will be guilty by association. You may say, "I don't smoke weed." But if you're riding in a car with three other guys who are smoking weed and the police pull you over, the driver rolls down the window, and all that smoke comes pouring out, the police aren't going to say, "We're taking all these guys in except for you." You may say, "I don't do crack." But if you go with someone you know to a crack house, and that house gets raided while you are there, you're going down with the rest of the people in that place. You will be guilty by association.

God wants us to have enough sense to know who to hang out with and who not to run around with. The Bible puts it like this: "Don't be yoked together with unbelievers" (2 Corinthians 6:14).

In other words, Christians should hang out with other Christians. People who know where they are going in life should hang out with other people who know where they are going in life. If you're smart, hang out with smart people; you can become even smarter. If your life has purpose and meaning, hang out with others whose lives have purpose and meaning.

Association brings about assimilation. Or, as Grandma used to put it, "If you lie down with dogs, you're going to wake up with fleas." Horses run with horses. Cows run with cows. Buffalo run with buffalo. Birds of a feather flock together. And a child of God who is on his way somewhere ought to hang out with other Christians who are on their way somewhere too. I know, son, that you can think of at least one intelligent person who was on his way somewhere, but got lost because of the crew he ran with. God wants something better for you.

Know When to Change Your Crew

Not everyone is a NASCAR fan, but you've probably heard of Jimmy Johnson, the great racecar driver. In 2009, he was in contention for the Sprint Cup Series Championship. There were three races to go in the series. Jimmy Johnson was doing well and had a good chance of winning. But in the Texas 500 his pit crew failed him. Typically, he would drive into a pit stop, and his crew would refuel the car; make any needed repairs; change the tires; and provide water for him as necessary.

But in this particular race, his crew was too slow. Each time he stopped, they delayed him from getting back onto the track quickly. During the third pit stop, they even dropped the lug nuts while changing a tire and were scrambling to get them picked up so that he could continue the race. This crew's failure caused a man who was ahead in the race to fall behind.

Even though this gifted and talented racecar driver had enjoyed previous victories and knew what he was doing, he couldn't win because of them. So, do you know what he did? Right in the middle of the race, he changed crews. Jeff Gordon, our Indiana homeboy who was on the same team as Johnson, had already crashed and was out of the race. But he had one of the best crews of the day. So Jimmy Johnson let his crew go and took Jeff Gordon's crew. He knew that they would give him an advantage. In those races, it isn't unusual to change one crew member, but it is very rare for a driver to change a whole crew in the middle of a race. Yet racecar drivers realize that their victory is dependent on the crew, so they've got to do what they need to do to win the victory.

Son, you may need to change your whole crew at times. I didn't keep the crew I was with in high school because some of them weren't going anywhere. I knew God had plans for my life, and I wanted to experience those plans. I knew that if I kept spending time with people who had no purpose, it wouldn't be long before I began feeling that way too. So when I went to college, I connected with guys who were close to God and who wanted to do something with their lives. They helped me to grow spiritually and encouraged me to keep following Christ.

Not All Dogs Are Male

God says that the people didn't have just wicked words and wayward ways. Proverbs 2:16 says, "Wisdom will save you also from the adulterous woman, from the wayward woman with her seductive words." In other words, wisdom will save you from the wrong woman. Aren't you glad God gives us wisdom? Now, the verse doesn't say wisdom will keep you from *all* women. It was God who came up with the concept of men and women. It was God who created humankind, male and female. It was God who put the first man and woman together and told them to reproduce. God has no objection to your finding a woman with whom you can spend your life. But He wants it to be the *right* woman. The truth is that marriage is hard enough with the *right* woman. It can get rough. It can be difficult. Just imagine how much harder it is if you are with the *wrong* woman.

Some sisters have the audacity to call brothers dogs. They say, "Aw, he's a dog," or "All men are dogs." But they only do that because they know brothers who have animalistic tendencies and beastly behavior. A Christian sister may even quote the Bible: "Even

Jesus said, 'Do not give what is holy to the dogs'" (Matthew 7:6 NKJV). But when Jesus said that, he wasn't just talking to women. He knows that not all dogs are male. There are female dogs, too. There are women who have animalistic tendencies and beastly behavior—even if they give the initial appearance of being too cute to hurt anyone. So the warning is the same. Don't take all that God has given to you and then go connect with a female dog, because she will eventually hurt you.

So then, how do you know right from wrong, a good woman from a bad woman? That's when God's wisdom is crucial. This scripture tells us the characteristics of a bad woman: she is adulterous, wayward, and uses seductive words. Proverbs 2:17 says that she does not live out the commitment to her husband; instead, "she has left the partner of her youth and ignored the covenant she made before God."

Keep in mind that Solomon was the one holding this conversation recorded here, and he had a thousand women in his life! He had seven hundred wives, along with three hundred women on the side. Yet after all his experiences with women, the advice he gave to his son was essentially, "Get yourself one good woman. That's all you need—just one good woman."

What Are You Looking For?

My question to you, son, is this: When you are looking for the right woman, what is the criteria that you use? I know that some men are so immature, all they think about is a woman's physical make-up. *Is she fine? That's all I care about. If she's fine, I can put up with everything else.* Now, I'm not mad at you for wanting her to be "fine." Even Adam was so impressed with Eve that he looked at her and said, "Wo-man! She's fine!" Well, he didn't actually use those words, but he viewed her differently from the other animals. She was part of him. Adam said, "This is now bone of my bones and flesh of my flesh; she shall be called 'woman,' for she was taken out of man" (Genesis 2:23). And Adam was no longer alone.

There is nothing wrong with wanting a woman who is fine. No one is going to tell you to go out and find the most unattractive woman you can and marry her, because this is the person you will be returning home to every evening. You want someone who is pleasing to look at. Men are stimulated by sight. When you get home, you want to see something that stimulates you. But also keep in mind that "beauty is in the eye of the beholder." If you think a woman is beautiful, then she is beautiful. Don't let someone else tell you what you are seeing through your own eyes.

But as you are determining the criteria by which you will select your wife, you must understand that "pretty" and "practical" are two different things. "Pretty" won't help you with fixing up that house. Pretty isn't going to sit with you in the hospital. Pretty isn't going to help you keep afloat financially by keeping within a budget or helping to increase the family income. Pretty doesn't cook. You need more than just "pretty."

No Room for Divorce

So you ask, "What is it that I need?" You need a woman who will keep her commitment to you as her husband. If you choose a woman who isn't willing to make that "till death do us part" commitment, then your marriage is never going to be all that it can be.

My wife and I have been married for twenty-six years. We haven't stayed married for that long because I've been a perfect husband and she's been a perfect wife. We haven't always naturally agreed on everything. We didn't have angels to come down from heaven and straighten out our arguments. We have had our issues and even major challenges just like every other married couple. But we were able to stay together because I chose a woman who understood commitment. We both came to the conclusion before we married that divorce is not an option. So, since we do not have that alternative to consider, we have to address whatever comes up within our home. We have to figure out how to make it work.

If you consider divorce an option, most likely you will make that your choice whenever things get rough. But when you are in a marriage for life, then you will work together on the issues because of the commitment that is there. And it isn't a matter of staying together just because you "have to." No! You don't want to be driving 'round and 'round the neighborhood because you dread going home. You want to work together with your spouse to create a home that is a refuge, a home that draws you into its comfort and warmth, a home in which you know you will find love and laughter.

The key to this type of commitment is that both you and the woman you marry must first have a covenant relationship with God. If a woman is in this type of a relationship with God, she understands commitment, even as you do. If she has committed her entire life to God, she will know what it means to commit her life to you as well. But if she can't love God right, what makes you think she can love you right? If she can't do right by God, who is perfect, how is she going to do right by you? You've got to choose the right woman.

Watch Out for the Tail

Do you remember Steve Irwin, the Crocodile Hunter? I loved watching him. When I watched him on TV, I didn't know at the time that he was an international celebrity. I didn't know how many countries carried his show or how popular he was around the globe. I just knew that I liked his show. He would go into a dark cave, pick up a poisonous snake by its tail, hold the snake, and almost get bit. "Oh!" he would say, "he almost got me, and had he bitten me, the poison would have gone into my bloodstream and I would have been dead in a few minutes." What he did was so adventurous and exciting. He would wrestle with alligators and crocodiles in the water, work with pythons and interact with all kinds of birds of prey. He was amazing. I've really missed him since he died.

You may already know that Steve Irwin died while filming a show about the deadliest creatures in the ocean. At the time he was swimming with stingrays, which are *not* among the deadliest creatures. In fact, they are known to be very docile. If you go to an aquarium, you are often allowed to pet the stingrays. So Steve Irwin was swimming with stingrays—a situation that should have been one of his safest experiences. But apparently, one of the stingrays must have thought that Steve was blocking him in, cornering him in a dead-end situation, and he reacted instinctively. He went into attack mode and stuck his tail into the Crocodile Hunter's chest. Some say this was a one-in-a-million shot, but it went right through Steve's heart.

Think about it: It wasn't dangerous crocodiles that killed Steve. It wasn't alligators that got him. It wasn't pythons, poisonous snakes, or birds of prey. What got him was a stingray's tail in his heart.

Son, I know you are bright. I know you have plans to get a Ph.D. I know you want to own your own company. I know you anticipate having a nice house and car. But if you're not careful, you won't reach your goals because you will end up with the wrong tail in your heart. I know you have overcome bullies, the absence of a father in your home, and a lot of social injustice. You have attained much and you have lofty goals for yourself. But if you're not careful, all your dreams could die unexpectedly from getting the wrong tail in your heart.

Get a Good Guide

Proverbs 2:20 (NLT) says, "Follow the steps of good men." You need to get a mentor—someone after whom you can model yourself, someone who can encourage you. . If you see it, you can be it; if you behold it, you can become it. Find a good man to follow who will serve as an example for you.

That verse continues, "And stay on the paths of the righteous." In other words, you need to walk in right ways—ways that are honest, moral, just, decent, and worthy of the One who called you. It's not enough to *talk* Christianity; we must also *walk* Christianity. When the Bible talks about "walking," it's referring to living a wholesome life that honors God in all that we do. It's not enough just to come to church, go through the motions of worship, and hear the Word of God being preached once a week. Instead, our Christian walk is about how we live our lives *every day* of the week. My childhood pastor used to say, "It's not how high you shout on Sunday. It's about how straight you come down and walk on Monday."

In Matthew 5:48 Jesus admonishes us, "Be perfect, therefore, as your heavenly Father is perfect." Thus, God expects a maturity in our behavior—to walk the way He has set before us. We adults have often judged our young people harshly on their walk. But their walk is so important because it says so much about them. When I see a young man walking down the street with his pants sagging and his behind showing, that just looks crazy to me. I know I'm fifty years old and from a different generation, but I don't understand why a young man would want to look that way. Some of today's teens retort that young men of my generation used to wear platform shoes. Yes, we did. But there is a difference between looking two inches taller and having your rear end showing. It's hard for some of us older folks to understand why young people walk as they do, why they dress in disarray on purpose, and why they act in ways that do not bring respect to themselves. But every generation talks about the generation following them, so you will someday talk about the young people you see and wonder why they behave as they do.

The Anger Factor

Another thing adults talk about is the anger of young people today. Even at thirteen years old, they appear so angry. At fourteen, they are mad at the world. They look like they would kill you if you accidentally bumped into them. So many older folks say, "I don't know why they look so angry."

I think I know why. If you watch your father walk out on you, it hurts so deeply that your feelings have to come out in some manner. For many children, the expression of those feelings involves showing anger. If you watch your momma work two jobs while your father isn't doing anything to help support you, you'll easily find anger welling up inside. If you watch men come and go in the life of your single mother without offering her a commitment, or if you watch a man beating her while you are too young to do anything to stop the abuse, the many mixed feelings inside you swirl into an angry force. If you watch a teacher look down upon you, or ignore you and assume that you will fail, that brings a pain that is often expressed in anger. If you watch store clerks eyeing you suspiciously just because you walk through the door, you can become angry. If you have security officers following you around for no reason, that produces anger. If you watch the flashing lights appear in your rearview mirror and know that you are being pulled over not for a traffic violation but simply for driving while black, that provokes anger.

The angry walk of young people that we adults are so quick to criticize is often the result of all the pain and woundedness they are carrying on the inside. What we see on the outside is a reflection of their broken spirits. Rather than criticizing them, we should try to help them.

Wounded People Don't Walk Well

Son, regardless of what the adults around you do, I want you to know that *God* can heal your wounds so you can start walking like a godly man. Recently I injured my leg while walking in my office. I was moving too fast and bumped into something immovable. When my leg collided with this object, the blood vessels in my leg burst and created a lot of pain. After the accident first happened, I literally couldn't walk. I actually had to hop to my car in order to drive to the hospital. When I got there, I couldn't park in a handicap spot because I don't have a handicap sticker. I had to park in a regular spot and start hopping into the hospital. Fortunately, someone inside the hospital saw me, came out with a wheelchair, and took me inside.

The doctor came into the room and began examining my leg. He asked me, "All of this happened because you bumped into something?"

"Yes."

"You must be on some kind of blood thinner or something."

"No, I don't take any blood thinner."

"Do you take aspirin or a similar type of medicine?"

"I don't take *any* medicine."

"I'm going to have to check your blood. Something seems to be wrong."

He had my blood tested, then came back and said, "Your blood is fine, but something isn't right here." He put an icepack on my leg and instructed the nurse to bandage it tightly. He told me, "You're going to have to elevate your leg and use these crutches. I'm going to write you a prescription, and if you feel any pain, take this medicine." Then he walked out of the room.

I said to the nurse, "Wait a minute. He didn't ask if I had any questions."

"Well, maybe I can answer them," she said.

The first thing I asked her was, "Will I be able to walk again?"

"Don't worry. You will be fine, but it's going to take some time."

I went to church the next Sunday and I did preach, but I had to stay in one spot because I couldn't walk. Then, when people were coming forward at the end of the service for prayer, I wasn't able to walk down the steps from the pulpit to the front of the sanctuary and later go back up. My leg was hurting so much that I couldn't do it. The next Sunday I was walking, but with an awkward limp and a grimace. (It's a long walk from my office to the pulpit.)

One of the brothers saw me and said, "Pastor, you've got your swag back." I said, "This isn't any swag. This is me suffering. And because I'm suffering, this is the only way I can walk in order to get to where I need to go. I'm not trying to be cool. I'm overcoming a crippling situation. I'm trying to overcome a fall." Adults are worried about the way our young men walk, when we ought to be worried about their wounds. If the wounds inside are healed, the walk will take care of itself.

God Heals Wounded Hearts

Son, I hear you asking, "So how do I do it? What do I do?" You know that your walk is messed up; your lifestyle is messed up. You know that you've not been dealing well with life and you've got a lot of anger pent up inside of you.

When the doctor walked out of the room without letting me ask any questions, the nurse offered to help. I said to her, "Well, he's given me a pill for the pain. He's given me an icepack and wrapped my leg to deal with the swelling. He's given me crutches to use to help me get around. But those things will just help treat the symptoms. None of this heals me. How am I going to be healed?"

She explained, "What happened was that you burst a lot of blood vessels in your leg. But the doctor said your blood is fine, and because your blood is fine, your body will reabsorb the blood."

Today, not only am I walking, but I'm leaping and I'm jumping. I've got my good walk back. Son, in terms of spiritual and emotional healing, Jesus' blood is still fine. It still has power. It still brings forgiveness. It still brings healing. The Lord can heal your wounds, and then your walk will take care of itself.

An Example to Consider: Daniel

Please take out your Bible and read Daniel 6.

There is a strange theology that some believe and some even preach. This teaching says that if we are Christians and stay true to God, nothing bad will ever happen to us. Where on earth does that belief come from? Certainly not from the Word of God! As we read the Bible, we see one after another of God's people who went through hard times. In fact, almost everyone whom God used in any mighty way went through difficult situations and trying times. Hopefully, you just read about Daniel. Think also of Abraham, Moses, Job, David, Paul, Silas, and, especially, Jesus.

Son, sometimes God protects us by preventing dangers from happening in our lives. However, there are times God protects us by preserving us as we go through difficulty. Daniel had to experience the lion's den, but he came through unhurt because God preserved him. Once he came through this experience, Daniel prospered. But even more, this experience caused King Darius to believe in Daniel's God, and he issued a proclamation telling the entire country that Daniel's God was the one true and living God. Had Daniel not gone through that experience, the king would not have seen the awesome reality and power of God, and none of those in the kingdom would have had an opportunity to learn about our God.

Sometimes we have to go *through* something in order for God to get us *to* something. And sometimes we have to go through something in order that God may be glorified. Romans 8:28 reminds us, "And we know that in all things God works for the good of those who love him, who have been called according to his purpose." Son, throughout your lifetime, God will bring you through one experience after another. He is always protecting you, even when you don't realize it. He always has your back. He is always there for you.

Dear God,

Thank You for loving me so much. Thank You that when I go through hard times, it doesn't have to mean that I have sinned and You are angry at me. Your Word offers so many examples of how Your people experienced various trials and tribulations along the way, and how You delivered them. For Daniel, You even sent an angel to close the mouths of the lions. Thank You, God, that what You did for Daniel, You can also do for me. Please deliver me from the lions in my life. Bring me forth in such a way that You are glorified. Thank You for not leaving me to face the lions alone. Thank You for Your deliverance. Thank You for Your love. Amen.

CHAPTER 3

Money Ain't a Thang

Honor the Lord with your wealth

and with the best part of everything you produce.

Then he will fill your barns with grain,

and your vats will overflow with good wine.

Proverbs 3:9-10, NLT

God Will Provide

One minister has suggested that if money is your problem, then you really don't have a problem—because money is not an issue for God. Haggai 2:8 says, "'The silver is mine and the gold is mine,' declares the Lord Almighty." Psalm 24:1 says, "The earth is the Lord's, and everything in it, the world, and all who live in it." The Lord owns all of it. Matthew 6:33 says, "But seek first his kingdom and his righteousness, and all these things will be given to you as well." If you seek first the kingdom of God—the rule of God, the reign of God—and His righteousness, then everything you need will be added to you. Jesus was speaking about housing, clothes, and food—the fundamental needs of life. You don't have to worry about them because God will provide them. So, if money is your problem, you don't really have a problem.

In Matthew 6:26, Jesus said, "Look at the birds of the air; they do not sow or reap or store away in barns, and yet your heavenly Father feeds them. Are you not much more valuable than they?" If God will watch over and feed these little animals with no souls and no relationship with Him, then what makes us think that God will not provide for our needs? The apostle Paul says, "And my God will meet all your needs according to the riches of his glory in Christ Jesus" (Philippians 4:19).

Money Is Good

You can start with the Book of Genesis and read through all the Bible, and what you will find is that there are a number of men to whom God has given so many material resources. God doesn't have an issue with our having money. Abraham, Isaac, Joseph, Solomon, David, Boaz, Nicodemus, and Joseph of Arimathea were all people with significant means. They all had money. God doesn't have a problem with our having money. The issue is not money itself. The problem comes because of our attitude toward money. It is a problem when we try to *acquire* money in the wrong way or *use* money in the wrong way. That is why the apostle Paul says, "The love of money is a root of all kinds of evil" (1 Timothy 6:10). It isn't the money itself, but the *love* of money that's dangerous.

We must have the right mindset about money, making sure that we are not putting money before God. God wants to be number one in your life and mine. When we pursue money, we have to do it in a way that is honorable to God. God doesn't want us stealing, killing, lying, manipulating, extorting, and dealing dishonestly with others. If God has something for us, we don't have to use those negative ways in order to get it. Money is not an issue with God.

When we read verses 5 and 6 of Proverbs 3, we find the voice of wisdom: "Trust in the Lord with all your heart and lean not on your own understanding; in all your ways submit to him, and he will make your paths straight." When we are living by God's Word, putting God first, and doing things God's way, wealth is not an issue. But if we do not have God's Word in our heads, He does not want to put His wealth in our hands.

The late Dr. Manuel L. Scott, Sr., who pastored Calvary Baptist Church in Los Angeles and then St. John Missionary Baptist Church in Dallas, said that you could put a dollar in the devil's hand and he would spend it wrong. It's not about the amount of money we have; it's a matter of the heart.

Choices, Not Chance

God has no issue with our possession of material resources, but, son, I want you to understand that it doesn't just happen by chance. You can't go through life thinking that you are somehow going to luck your way into prosperity. It doesn't happen by chance. The choices you and I make, as they agree with God's Word and will, are the determining factors in whether or not we will have money.

The Indianapolis Colts had the number one pick in the 2012 NFL Draft, and they drafted Andrew Luck. What a great pick! He is indeed a great football player, a great quarterback. We saw what he had done at Stanford and how he helped to turn that program around. He has passion for the game and leadership ability. He is a young man with intelligence, strength, and skill. He is accurate with a pass, but not only can he pass, he can also run. So, Luck was a great pick. But what we are learning from the Indianapolis Colts is that if we are going to get the ultimate victory, Luck alone won't be enough. We are all going to need more than luck to get the ultimate victory. We are going to need some good coaching, some strategies, a plan, some goals, some cooperative teammates, and a playbook. If we think we're going to win with just luck, we'll find that's not enough.

Here's the thing I'm trying to get across to you: If you are looking for financial stability, financial freedom, and financial victory, you can't rely just on luck. You need to get together with somebody who understands money management. You need someone who can help you to learn about investment strategies, insurance, and retirement planning. You need someone who can coach you and help you to develop a plan and set goals. You will need a cooperative teammate. If a husband is doing one thing with the family's income to reach one set of goals, and the wife is doing something else to reach another set of goals, there is no way they are going to have financial victory.

It Is Written

Your plan needs to be a written plan, so that you, your wife, and children all understand the plan and are working together accordingly to make it happen. You write down that you are giving a certain percentage of your income to God; putting a certain percentage in savings; investing a certain percentage in retirement; and spending a certain percentage on housing, food, school expenses, transportation, and other needs. Then you set aside a little money for entertainment, vacation planning, and other things you want to do. The whole family can then see how the family's income is going to be allocated, and they can all be on the same page. Again, you must understand that financial prosperity isn't going to happen with just luck.

You also need a playbook. The greatest playbook you can get to help you towards financial understanding, freedom, and victory is the Bible. If you open it, read it, and let God speak to you, you will find that He has a wonderful playbook that will put you on the road to financial success.

Remember: when it comes to God, money ain't a thang. Money ain't a thang when you pay God first. Proverbs 3:9 tells us to honor God with our wealth. We have to pay God first. The word "honor" comes from the same root word as "honorarium." An honorarium is money paid to someone for something that person has done. We need to honor the Lord Jehovah, the One with whom we have entered into a relationship through His Son Jesus Christ, by paying Him from our wealth. The word "wealth" actually means "enough." We must pay the Lord with "enough."

Putting God First

The next verse tells us what will happen when we do that. Proverbs 3:9-10 says, "Honor the Lord with your wealth, with the firstfruits of all your crops; then your barns will be filled to over-flowing, and your vats will brim over with new wine." In our terms, it means that our bank account will be filled to overflowing and our lives will spill over with joy and celebration. But none of that will happen if we don't first honor the Lord with our wealth, with enough. So, we have to ask ourselves, "If our barns are empty and our vats are dry, have we given God enough?" God already owns it all, so if *our* stuff is empty and dry, the issue is not with God.

If I find myself in that situation, I have to ask myself, *Jeffrey Johnson, have you given God enough?* How do I know if it is enough? How do I know what enough is? I know because the Bible tells me that I should be giving God a tithe and an offering. God tells me in Malachi 3:10: "'Bring the whole tithe into the storehouse, that there may be food in my house. Test me in this,' says the Lord Almighty, 'and see if I will not throw open the floodgates of heaven and pour out so much blessing that there will not be room enough to store it.'" The tithe belongs to God. If I haven't given God a tithe, then I haven't given God enough. My finances can be messed up because I haven't given God enough. The tithe is ten percent. It is a representation of the whole. So, when I give God ten percent, I am recognizing that He owns the whole. By giving my tithe, I am demonstrating that I know it is all His. I am saying to God, "I am giving You a tithe, which is a sign that my faith is in You."

Also notice that in Proverbs 2:9, it doesn't say just bring in *any* of your crops. It says bring God your "firstfruits." That means, bring Him your *best*. God deserves the first and the finest, not the least and the leftovers. When we get an increase, God wants His share off the top. He doesn't want to wait until we've wasted our money on all kinds of junk and then give Him a piddly little amount that means nothing to us or to Him. If we make two thousand dollars and buy all kinds of needless things for ourselves, we had better not bring our leftover two dollars to church and talk about giving our *all* to

God. That isn't your "all." That's just all you've got left. God isn't looking for all we've got left. He wants His share *first*.

When the Bible was written, it was addressed primarily to people who were farmers and shepherds. They had crops, flocks of sheep, herds of cattle, and other things that we would find in that agricultural setting. That is what they got as a result of their labor. Therefore, when they came to the temple, that's what they brought as their tithes and offerings. They didn't bring checks, get cash from an ATM to bring, have a transfer made directly from a bank account, or put money into an envelope and drop it into an offering plate. No, they went to their flock or herd and brought an animal. They went to their farms and brought the crops they had grown.

They also brought their animals to offer as a sacrifice to God. They would shed the animal's blood, take a portion of it, and burn it. That's where the term "burnt offering" comes from. The smoke that arose from the offering would go up to God and it was a sweet aroma that let God know of their faith in Him. So they had to go, look among their sheep, find the biggest and the best and bring that one to God. If they had cattle, they would find the finest calf in the herd to bring to God.

What God was saying through Malachi in the Old Testament is that too many people were selecting animals that were blind, lame, or diseased and bringing them as offerings to God. God essentially told them, "No. You want to bring Me something that you can't use.

I don't want your leftovers. I want your best. I don't want you to give Me something that costs you nothing."

The animals that were sacrificed in Old Testament times were symbolic of the sacrifice that Jesus would make later on when He went to the cross and died for our sins. When God sent Jesus to earth to die for our sins, He was sending His best. John 3:16 (KJV) says, "For God so loved the world that he gave his only begotten son . . ." Because God gave us His best, He has a right to expect us to give Him our best in return. So, when we are giving our tithes and offerings to God, we have to ask ourselves, *Is this our best?* If it's our best and finest, then our barns will overflow and our vats will be brimming with joy, celebration, life, and prosperity. If not, our barns will be empty and our vats will be dry. Money ain't a thang when we pay God first.

Learn from Their Mistakes

One night I was watching a special on ESPN from their "30 for 30" series—thirty films to commemorate ESPN's thirtieth anniversary. This film, entitled "Broke," explored the lives of former professional athletes who had made tens of millions of dollars but a few years later found themselves broke. They are now bankrupt, in debt, and have no money at all.

Now, son, I already know what you are thinking. *If I had all that money, I would never go broke. If I had 35 million dollars, I'd never be bankrupt.* But wait a minute. What strategy are you going to use? What's your plan? Who's your coach? What playbook are you using? You earned thirty-five thousand dollars last year, and you blew it. If you can blow thirty-five thousand dollars, you sure can't manage 35 million dollars. What you do with a little is an indication of what you are going to do with a lot. That's why God says if we can't handle a little, He isn't going to give us a lot. But if we prove that we are faithful with the little He gives us, He will entrust more into our hands. (See Matthew 25:14-29.)

But in that special, there were those athletes who had millions of dollars going through their hands, and nothing to show for it. I appreciated the honesty of some of them who want to keep other young people from making the same mistakes. Some said that they made bad investments or had trusted the wrong person with their money. Oprah Winfrey has said, "When you own your own company, sign your own checks." But some of these guys had put their money into someone else's hands, and now they have nothing to show for it.

Then they started talking about all that they had bought, including houses, cars, SUVs, jewelry, and trips. One of them had taken a trip to go to a particular store, where he spent over a quarter of a million dollars on jewelry. They talked about their entourage—ten, twenty, or thirty people who tagged along with them everywhere they went. Sometimes they didn't even know who all those people were. But everywhere they all went, these millionaires paid for everything.

117

One of them said, "If we flew, I paid for that. If we went to eat at an expensive restaurant, I paid for that. If we made it rain at a strip club, I paid for that." They paid for everything and now they are broke.

One thing that especially interested me is what they *didn't* say. I watched it twice to make sure I wasn't missing it. Not one of them said anything like, "I established a foundation for the poor to make sure the least, the lonely, and the poor have opportunities for education, housing, and job training. I lost my money trying to make sure the poor were taken care of." None of them said anything like that. Of course, that doesn't surprise me because they couldn't have gone broke doing that. Proverbs 19:17 says, "Whoever is kind to the poor lends to the Lord, and he will reward them for what they have done." God would have been making it rain on them if they had been using their money to care for the poor.

None of the athletes interviewed in that program said, "I became broke by giving all of my money to the church or to missions to further God's kingdom in the world. I love God and want others to know Him in a personal way like I do, so I gave my money to help make that happen." None of them said that. Of course, that doesn't surprise me because Big Momma 'n 'em were right: "You can't beat God giving. You can't out give God." The more we give to God, the more He gives to us.

In fact, the way you can get out of a financial crisis is by paying God first. Remember Malachi 3:10, which I quoted for you earlier: "'Bring the whole tithe into the storehouse, that there may be food in my house. Test me in this,' says the Lord Almighty, 'and see if I will not throw open the floodgates of heaven and pour out so much blessing that there will not be room enough to store it.'" If you give little, you get little back; but if you give generously, you will get so much back that you won't be able to contain it all. Money ain't a thang when you pay God first.

Nobody Owes You Anything

Money ain't a thang when you are pragmatic, practical. Let me be clear. Money ain't a thang when you work. You cannot go through life, son, with a mentality of entitlement. You can't believe that somebody owes you something. Some men say foolish things like, "I didn't ask to be born, but since I'm here, somebody owes me something," "I'm not workin', but my granddaddy worked and paid taxes, so I've got somethin' comin' to me," or even, "Look, I graduated from high school, went on to college, and got a degree; now somebody owes me a job."

Son, there is nobody who feels that they owe you anything. Nobody. No employers hire anyone because they feel that they *owe* somebody a job. They hire an individual because they feel that person will be the best fit for the position they have open. That man or woman will be the best at helping their business or organization to succeed. If they don't think you can help them make money or help them accomplish their mission, they aren't going to hire you.

Employers do not hire employees to help the employees. They hire employees to help *them*. No one will hire you out of the goodness of their heart. They don't feel that they owe you anything.

In fact, I heard someone say recently on a television program that the older you get, the less likely folks want to help you. So, let's say you are fifteen or sixteen years old and you've come from a broken home and a difficult childhood. Someone might say, "Okay, let's help this boy get a start in life. Let's give him a chance." Or, if you are twenty-two years old and just out of college, someone might say, "Okay, you've really been working hard. You've been trying to help yourself, so I'm going to open a door for you."

But now you're twenty-nine. You've quit two jobs. You don't have a good track record. The response you get is, "Uh, yeah . . . call me sometime. I'll try to hook you up." Or now, you're forty-two—and no one even takes your calls. The older you get and the more spotty your work record, the less likely people are to help you get a job. Finding a job isn't about entitlement. It's about using your energy, your effort, and your work to show that you are worthy of the job.

Look again at Proverbs 3:9-10: "Honor the Lord with your wealth, with the firstfruits of all your crops; then your barns will be filled to overflowing, and your vats will brim over with new wine." Notice that this is not wealth that has come without work. It didn't mean a farmer could be standing out in a field and, all of a sudden, crops sprang up, and grapes jumped off the vine and into a winepress where they became wine. No, it is about hard work. This is a reference to farmers, who cleared their fields, plowed their lands, sowed their seed, dug trenches to create an irrigation system, weeded their crops, and eventually gathered in a harvest. This took time, energy, and a lot of continuous effort. They also had to put up fences around their land to keep wild animals from coming in and devouring their crops. They had to pick the grapes, put the grapes into the press, stomp on the grapes to get the juice, and then build channels for the juice to flow into the vats. All of this was hard work. These verses were not talking about getting wealth without working.

This passage also was not referring to work without training. A person doesn't automatically know how to operate a vineyard just because he or she buys land with that in mind. A farmer has to learn when and how to sow, how to water, and how to care for the grapes.

Whatever you are going to do in life, son, you have to *learn* how to do it. You have to find someone to teach you. Learning is for everybody. Whether it happens in college, a vocational/technical school, or through an apprenticeship, there has to be a time when you learn what you need to know to be able to have something to offer in this world. You must have knowledge, ability, or a skill in order to help in some endeavor. Whether you are going to start your own business or go to work for somebody else, you need something to bring to the table. The bigger the problem you can solve, the more someone will be willing to pay you. People will not pay you, however, when you *are* the problem. You can only get the wealth when you solve the problem and do the work.

Work: Blessing or Curse?

God worked six days and rested on the seventh. Since we are created in God's image, we should at least put in six days of work. Remember that if you want to know how something should be done, you go back to the first time God did it. Adam was not simply *a* man; he was *the* man—the only one. When God created Adam, He put him to work in the garden. Now, some people say that Adam didn't start working in the garden until after he sinned, and work was part of the curse he had to endure in his sinful state. But whoever says that is just plain wrong.

Let's go back and see what the Bible says about this. It isn't until chapter 3 of Genesis that we read about Adam's sin. But Genesis 2:15 says, "The Lord God took the man and put him in the Garden of Eden to work it and take care of it." So Adam was working the garden and caring for it before Eve, before the fall, and before the curse. Adam's work was, in fact, twofold. He used his intelligence to name all of the animals, and he used his physical energy and strength to care for the garden. Adam's life had purpose and meaning. Work was not a curse; it was a blessing.

The curse, which came later, was that Adam had to work twice as hard and had less to show for it. That's a curse. If I am working twelve hours a day, seven days a week and I have nothing to show for it, that's a curse. Work itself is not a curse. The Bible says if we don't work, we shouldn't eat. To the church of the Thessalonians, Paul wrote, "For even when we were with you, we gave you this rule: 'The one who is unwilling to work shall not eat' " (2 Thessalonians 3:10). In fact, prior to that verse, he wrote in 2 Thessalonians 3:8-9:

> For you yourselves know how you ought to follow our example. We were not idle when we were with you, nor did we eat anyone's food without paying for it. On the contrary, we worked night and day, laboring and toiling so that we would not be a burden to any of you. We did this, not because we do not have the right to such help, but in order to offer ourselves as a model for you to imitate.

Paul had set an example before the church as one who "worked night and day, laboring and toiling" as a model for the church to imitate.

Who's Your Momma?

Those who will not work are trying to live off the labor of somebody else. If you are not working, then who is paying for your rent, buying your food, and putting gas in your car? Are you living off the labor of your mother? Your father? Remember, the older you get, the less folk are inclined to help you. At some point, Momma's going to stop helping you. At some point, Daddy's going tell you to go out on your own.

A guy with that lazy mindset still doesn't get it. He still doesn't go out, get a job, and make something of his life. Instead, he finds a girlfriend and moves in with her. He stays with her until she gets tired of the freeloading and kicks him out. Then he finds another girlfriend—someone so lonely and needy that she's willing to take care of him like a little boy, instead of being a woman who knows she is worthy of a mature man who will love her and work with her to build a life together.

The fool living with her is so immature and insensitive that he goes around bragging to his boys, "She bought me this. She got me that. She did this for me." That's not a sign of manhood. Being able to manipulate a woman and use her to get what he wants is not anything to be proud of.

But he keeps looking for that woman who is so desperate that she will even marry him while he is not working—thinking that she will be able to change him after they get married. She erroneously thinks that he isn't working because he doesn't have any responsibilities, but that after he is married, he will feel responsible and will go to work. She doesn't understand that he has had responsibilities all along. He should have been working and meeting his responsibilities before they even met. He should have been providing for his own shelter, buying his own food, and paying for his own clothes all along. But if he wasn't working then, what makes her think he will go to work now? He won't. Entering into a marriage with someone who will not work is outside the will of God.

Job or No Job, We Work

Notice that I have been very careful to use the word "work," not the word "job." I'm talking about having a good work ethic. I realize how messed up our economy can be and how bad the job market can be. I know that many people—men and women—have skills, education, and ability but don't have a job. I understand how bad things can be. But those with a strong work ethic will work even if they don't have a job. For people who have the discipline to work, a job will eventually come along.

Moses is a prime example of this. He was born into a poor and persecuted minority family. But God kept His hand on Moses and worked things out so that he ended up in Pharaoh's household. He was trained as a prince, had an Egyptian education, and was exposed to the African culture and its customs. He was next in line to be the king of Egypt. He went from poverty to prosperity. But then, he messed up his situation. He had no one else to blame. (Read about it in Exodus 2:11-21.) Instead of staying in the palace and working, he went out to watch other people work. He ended up killing somebody. He lost his position, became afraid for his life, and fled to another country. He was a wanted man who was unemployed, with no transportation and no references. The only things he owned were the clothes on his back.

Moses was hanging out in Midian and happened to be at a well when seven sisters came to draw water for their father's flock. They were working. He saw some other shepherds come along and try to drive them away from the well. Now, Moses was unemployed, but he still had a work ethic and he still had some integrity left. So, he took on the thugs who were attacking the women and drove them away. Then he watered the women's flock himself.

When the women got home early, their father asked them how they were able to water the animals and get back so early. They told him about this man who protected them from the thugs and then watered the flock himself. Their father was impressed with what Moses had done. He told his daughters to go find the man and bring him back home. Moses got both a job and a wife because of the person he was on the inside. To someone looking only on the outside, he appeared to be a homeless drifter, but he was actually a hard-working man. He still had a work ethic even though he had no job at the time he met Jethro's family. The work ethic prompted him to work to water the flock even though it was not his job and he was not getting paid to do it. The work he did was honorable, and it brought its own reward.

The Benefits of Ownership

Work is not a curse. It is a blessing. We should thank God that we have the strength and health to be able to work. Most find work more rewarding when they are not simply going to a job every day, but instead, they own their own businesses. They are proprietors, entrepreneurs. They get to cast the vision for their workplace, make the operational decisions, and have a greater potential for wealth. Nobody else is going to pay you the way *you* will pay you. As long as you are working for someone else, you will never get what you think you need or deserve.

Remember that Proverbs 3 was speaking to a farmer, a land-owner, the owner of a vineyard. It wasn't a day laborer receiving this advice. It was someone who had bought land, cleared the land, planted crops and a vineyard. He developed the land by building barns and other facilities. This was a business owner. When he harvested the crops and sold the produce and the wine, the profits would all be his. He would be able to reinvest into his business and grow his wealth potential.

In the same way, we should not limit our own potential. We should not be content to simply be a "worker" when we can be an "owner." God often has a greater vision for us than we have for ourselves. God sees the potential within us and knows what He is able to accomplish through us. Sometimes we hold ourselves back because we fall into ways that are comfortable and familiar, and we never get to see our barns filled and our vats overflowing as they might if we could catch the vision God has for us.

Going to school and getting a job can give us a paycheck, but owning our own business allows us to acquire wealth. When you own your own stuff, you get equity. There is value in your property, and it is all yours.

You Choose

Let's say that you go to school and get a degree. You come out and go to work for a small company that makes a million dollars a year. They hire you and pay you forty-five thousand dollars a year. That's good money for someone right out of school.

Now, let's look at the situation three years later. The company is bringing in four million dollars a year. You have worked hard to get them to that point. Your skills, intelligence, ability, management expertise, and commitment have helped to build that company. So, now they are paying you seventy-five thousand a year. That's really good money. You've been out of school for just three years and are making seventy-five thousand dollars. That's good money. But the company is bringing in four million a year, and you are getting only a small portion of that amount. And while the company has an equity of two million dollars, you don't get *any* of that. You don't own the company. You're just an employee.

Now, let's fast forward. Seventeen years later, the company is bringing in $25 million and is now valued at $30 million. Of course, the owner recognizes that you helped to make the company what it is and appreciates you and your work, so he is paying you two hundred and fifty thousand dollars a year. You're in the top three-percent income bracket in the country. They also have given you a lot of perks along the way: good insurance, a good retirement program, ample vacation days, NBA season tickets, NFL season tickets, a new leased company car every three years, and a trip every year for you and your family to anywhere in the United States. They are taking good care of you because you helped this company grow from a one-million dollar company to a $30 million corporation. They value you, so they reward you.

But what you don't fully grasp is that you are working just as hard as the owner. A lot of the ideas that moved the company forward were your ideas. In terms of your time, talent, and energy, you are as fully invested as the owner. But while you are getting money, the owner is getting wealth. He is gaining equity. He is gaining the full value of the company. But you are still happy because you are making good money.

But let's go a few years even further into the future. Now you've been with the company for twenty years. The owner decides he wants a change. Concerned about the people of Haiti, he wants to develop a nonprofit to help the people of that country. He has spent much of his life gaining wealth, and now he wants to spend the rest of his life doing something that will give his life greater meaning and purpose. He wants to be able to leave a legacy that is measured in more ways than simply dollar signs, so he decides to sell the business. He makes the sale and gets $30 million. He gives you a generous severance package of three hundred thousand dollars. You are happy. That's a lot of money, and it will help you to keep going until you land your next position.

But think about it. He gets $29,700,000. And when you stop to reflect over the past twenty years, you remember that he wasn't always even at the job. He told you countless times that he knew he could trust you, so he stayed home or engaged in other activities while you kept the company growing. You were happy at the time that you were trusted enough to handle the business. But now, he walks away with almost $30 million and you only have three hundred thousand. He was the owner. You were the employee. He can retire, relax, regroup, and reinvest. You, on the other hand, need to find another job because three hundred thousand dollars isn't going to take you to retirement. You have a family to provide for, children to put through college, a car to buy on your own, a need for insurance, and a lot of expenses that come along with living the lifestyle to which you and your family are accustomed. Think about the difference between the two of you.

Vision, Not Fantasy

Now, son, I know that you may not be getting into this scenario. While I'm talking about academics and economics, and trying to get you to understand the difference between money and wealth, you aren't interested in any of that. The reason might be that, like so many young men today, you don't have a *vision* for your life, but a *fantasy* instead. When one of the men in our church asked a group of young boys what they were going to be when they grew up, they actually started talking about superheroes. One said he was going to be Batman; another was going to be Superman. They all had great imaginations, but no grasp of reality.

Often the mindset of teenage boys is no better. They think they are going to be a great rapper or a top NBA basketball player. Really, son, do you think that at five foot ten, you are going to be the next Kobe Bryant? And you know that you can't hear a beat and have trouble putting two sentences together. Do you really think you are going to have your name written alongside Jay-Z's? Son, I'm not being negative about you. You are intelligent. You possess some extraordinary personal qualities. You have talents and gifts. You were born for greatness. But what I am suggesting is that you widen your interests and broaden your boundaries. Don't limit your vision to the world of celebrities.

Think about the numbers. Consider how few men are good enough to play professional ball of any type. I love playing basketball and was a decent player in my little world, but I knew better than to think that I could make it a career. Even if God hadn't called me to preach when I was seventeen years old, I wouldn't have been spending my time making free throws and practicing 3-pointers. I knew that I would have had about as much chance playing for the NBA as I would have of being transformed into Batman, my personal favorite superhero. I had enough sense to know the difference between vision and fantasy. I didn't want a fantasy that would leave me empty, unfulfilled, and defeated. I wanted a vision for my life that would enable me to walk in God's plan for me. Once I knew that plan included preaching, I spent my time trying to become a better preacher, a good leader, and a more Christ-like person.

Son, God had a purpose for your life when He created you. Let Him reveal that purpose to you. Let Him give you a vision that you can embrace with His blessing, and then keep moving in the direction of that vision. You may not see the whole picture right now, but just take the next step in the direction you believe God wants you to go. Those single steps will eventually get you there.

It Takes Time

Money ain't a thang when we realize it takes a certain period of time to make it all happen. When the scripture says that your barns will be filled and your vats will overflow with wine, it recognizes that it takes time to produce wine. And the longer the time, the more

132

valuable the wine. We have too many people who want to be grape juice Christians and grape juice money- makers. God has something more in mind for us. God is talking about wine—something of value, something that represents prosperity. It takes time to produce any crop. You cannot sow corn one day and have a field of corn the next. It takes time. You can't plant grape seeds one day and have a vineyard the next. No, it takes time.

Son, stop trying to start where your mom and dad left off. Your mother and father took thirty to forty years to get that house, own that property, possess those stocks and bonds, get that car, buy those clothes, and be able to take those great vacations. It took them at least thirty years to get to that point. You've been out of school three years and think that you should have all that right now. No, it's going to take time. Stop trying to find a get-rich-quick scheme. Stop thinking that you're going to win the lottery. Stop thinking that somehow overnight you are going to get rich. That mindset makes you vulnerable to any shyster that comes along. Some unscrupulous person talks you into investing in a pyramid scheme and you think, *It sounds too good to be true*. It IS too good to be true! Stop believing the fantasy!

Do you know how many people have approached me with pyramid schemes? I've been pastoring Eastern Star Church for twenty-four years, and every single year, at least one person has approached me with a new pyramid scheme.

"Pastor, can I talk to you?"

"What's it about?"

"I've got a business idea. I know how to help the church get money, and I can make you rich."

First of all, I look at the person and say, "You aren't rich. You go get rich first and then come back and we can talk about how you can help me to get rich."

This person came to me because he has two friends and three family members. I have seventeen thousand church members. So, what he is thinking is that if I come in under him on the pyramid scheme, and seventeen thousand people follow under me, it will make both of us rich. But I point out to him that if all that were true, I wouldn't need him at all. I'm the one with the seventeen thousand people, so I don't need him. His mentality is so messed up. It's all so crazy. And yet, every day some vulnerable people buy into such a scheme and end up losing the little money that they do have.

Son, you cannot rush wealth. It takes time. It takes discipline. It takes planning. It takes training. It takes faith in God. It takes faithfulness for me to do what I am doing now. I have to keep going to work early. I have to keep striving for excellence in my work. I have to keep praying. I have to keep trusting God and worshiping Him. I have to keep on believing Him. There has to be consistency in my walk. Even to this day, I am still reaping rewards from those things I did twenty years ago. Sometimes, someone will see what I'm reaping right now, and they get envious and angry. But that person hasn't seen what I've gone through the past twenty years. He didn't see the sacrifices I made twenty years ago. He only sees what I am reaping now. I didn't invest in some get-rich-quick scheme. I decided I was going to trust God over time. Seed, time, and harvest. I decided I was going to seed to my need, trust God over time, and wait for my harvest.

Seed What You Need

Son, what is it that you need? Whatever you need, seed to that, because you reap what you sow. If you need apples, you don't plant orange seeds. If you need love, then be more loving. If you need friends, then be more friendly. If you need respect and honor, be sure that you respect and honor others. If you need a healthier relationship, then stop sowing craziness into the relationship you are in. If you need money, sow money.

God says to honor the Lord with your wealth if you want your own barns and vats to overflow. Remember, Malachi 3:10 says, "'Bring the whole tithe into the storehouse, that there may be food in my house. Test me in this,' says the Lord Almighty, 'and see if I will not throw open the floodgates of heaven and pour out so much blessing that there will not be room enough to store it.'" You reap what you sow, but it all takes time. Yet, as gospel singer Dottie Peoples sings, "He's an on-time God, yes, He is." In the meantime, while you are waiting for the harvest, you have to be consistent. You have to keep sowing, keep tending your crop, keep trusting, and keep waiting patiently.

Consumer or Producer?

Money ain't a thang when you learn how to produce. One thing that trips us up is that we are better consumers than we are producers. In this portion of Scripture, they are producing food from their crops and wine from their grapes. They produce what other people need. When you produce what other people need, you are on your way to prosperity. When all you do is need what other people produce, you are on your way to poverty. Some of us are great consumers. In fact, all we know how to do is consume. We buy clothes that wear out. We buy cars that depreciate in value. We buy the latest fads that are quickly outdated. We consume, and consume, and consume.

Because we are made in the image of God, we have imagination inherent within us. But when was the last time that you used your imagination to create or produce something? We are more like God when we produce. We are more like the enemy, when we consume. . He comes but to kill, steal and destroy. (See John 10:10.) We have to be producers, not mere consumers.

When was the last time that you came up with an idea of a service for which people would pay you? How long has it been since you've thought of a product you could make that people would buy from you? We are great consumers, but terrible producers. That's why money is always an issue for us.

In 2012 African Americans earned in excess of $800 billion. Then we spent $48.5 billion on new cars and trucks, $23.5 billion on clothes, $11 billion on furniture to put in a rented apartment, $3 billion on electronics, and $3 million on books. We went out and bought $3 *billion* worth of Xboxes and Playstations and various video games, but spent only $3 *million* on books. We make up just twelve percent of our nation's population yet bought thirty percent of the Scotch that was sold. We are great consumers. Of those of us who earn a hundred thousand dollars or more a year, 30 percent don't have even five thousand dollars set aside in a retirement program. We are great consumers, but have yet to learn how to produce. We have yet to learn the difference between money and wealth.

You Gotta Know Your Options

LeBron James was drafted by the Cleveland Cavaliers at eighteen, so he was in the highest pay bracket that a rookie could make. When his next contract came up, however, he turned down the extra $20 million because he wanted to be a free agent. After seven years in Cleveland, he said he was taking his talent to South Beach.

At that point the mainstream mass media decided they didn't like LeBron James. It didn't matter to them that he came from a broken home, overcame issues regarding his mother, worked really hard and disciplined himself, got MVP awards as he helped his team win games, hung out with people like Warren Buffet to learn entrepreneurial skills as he started his own business, and acted like a mature and responsible adult. They still didn't like him. The same ones who sang his praises were now putting him down. So, what changed? People said it was because he was taking his talents to South Beach, but that wasn't the real reason.

The real reason was economics. It was all about money and wealth. Dan Gilbert, the owner of the Cavaliers at the time, became very negative about him leaving, lamenting, "After all I did for LeBron James." When LeBron got drafted by Cleveland, the team was worth $200 million. Seven years later, it was worth $450 million. When LeBron left, he got zero from the $450 million because he only received money from his basketball-related activities. He had no stake in the equity or value of the team itself. Only the owner got the $450 million. Here, this man said he was mad at LeBron, even though the star player was chiefly responsible for increasing the value of his team by $250 million in just seven years.

What many folks didn't like, quite honestly, was the fact that this Black man was making decisions for himself. He was simply an employee who had the right to decide to move elsewhere for another job, just like an employee of any other company. But some people didn't want him to have that mentality. They wanted him to feel compelled by some false sense of loyalty to stay in his place, where he was making money for them and drawing attention to their team and their city. But although LeBron was getting excellent pay and recognition, he still was just an employee.

Dan Gilbert was the owner of the Cavaliers. He got $450 million. Players saw and understood the difference. That's why when Magic Johnson, Michael Jordan, and Larry Bird finished being employees, they wanted to own their own franchises. They wanted to own something for themselves instead of just making money for somebody else. They understood wealth in contrast to money.

Perseverance, Not Perfection

Son, money ain't a thang when you stop dropping out. We drop out of high school. We drop out of college. We drop out of healthy relationships. We drop out of functional friendships. We drop out of marriage. We drop out of raising our children. We drop out of jobs. There are twenty-two-year-olds who have had eight different jobs. If you ask why, they'll say, "They didn't like me over there," "They are prejudiced over there," "They don't like Black people," or "They've got issues." I don't care where you go to get a job, somebody isn't going to like you. Somebody will be racist. Somebody will be prejudiced. Somebody will find something wrong with you.

But I personally would not quit a job because somebody doesn't like me. I didn't get the job in order that someone would like me. *I* like me. My mortgage and my children's college tuition like me. What I'm saying, son, is that life isn't easy or fair. But we aren't quitters. We want to experience all that God has for us, so we keep on doing what we know is right in God's sight and let God handle the rest.

While my son, Jalon, was hanging out in Atlanta with our oldest son, Jay, he texted his mother and me a picture of a church he saw. The name of it was "The Perfect Church." My wife Sharon texted back, "Did you go to the church?"

"No, we didn't go there."

"Why not?"

"Well, Daddy always said that if you find a perfect church, don't go in there, because you're going to mess it up."

Son, if you are looking for the perfect job, the perfect wife, the perfect marriage, the perfect college, the perfect family, just take a picture of it and text it to me. Don't go in there because you are going to mess it up. Everybody's got issues. You are not going to find a perfect situation. But you do have a perfect God, a perfect Savior, and you can have a right relationship with Him. And when you get that, money ain't a thang.

An Example to Consider: Shamgar

(Please take out your Bible and read Judges 3:31.)

The Bible has so many stories that go on for chapter after chapter, telling of the exploits of the heroes and heroines who did great things for God. Even Othniel and Ehud in Judges 3 have some details in their stories that make them seem interesting and significant. But in comparison to all of these, Shamgar didn't seem to have a lot to offer. In the entire Bible, only two lines are devoted to his actions and his role in the life of God's people.

But that second line says, "He too saved Israel." Think about it. He too saved Israel—God's chosen people, the people through whom the Messiah would one day come. Shamgar saved Israel.

Did he do this through a magnificent plan of battle? Did he bring forth a host of armies to fight against the enemy? Did he rally the people to march around a city until the walls fell down so they could go in and overtake the enemy? No, he struck down six hundred Philistines with an ox goad, which is a long stick with a pointed end that was used to prod animals along. Shamgar saved Israel with a stick.

In the words of Dr. A. Louis Patterson, Jr., pastor of Mount Corinth Missionary Baptist Church in Houston, "Shamgar started where he was, used what he had, and did what he could." As a result, God did great things through his life. Son, you cannot start where you are not present. You cannot use what you do not have. And you cannot do what you cannot do. Just be the unique person God made you. Allow the power of God's Holy Spirit to empower you, and remember that you can do all things through Christ who strengthens you. God has all the resources you need.

Dear God,

I'm sorry for the times that I have fantasized about doing great things for You while I haven't even been willing to do the little things You've asked of me. I'm sorry for thinking that my gifts and talents are too small or insignificant to be of value in Your kingdom. I'm sorry for hiding my talent instead of using it because I was afraid. I'm sorry for not doing anything that requires real faith, and instead doing only those things that I knew I could handle. I'm sorry for limiting Your power in my life. I yield myself to You afresh and anew and ask You to forgive me, empower me, and strengthen me to be the man You had in mind when You created me. In the name of my Savior, I pray. Amen.

CHAPTER 4

Get Your Mind Right

My child, pay attention to what I say.

Listen carefully to my words.

Don't lose sight of them.

Let them penetrate deep into your heart,

for they bring life to those who find them,

and healing to their whole body.

Guard your heart above all else,

for it determines the course of your life.

(Proverbs 4:20-23 NLT)

A Lot of Craziness

My mother has accused me on more than one occasion of calling everybody crazy. If something negative would happen in the community, I would say about the person responsible, "That person's crazy." If I heard something on the news about someone bringing harm to somebody else, I might say, "That person's crazy." If I heard about something happening politically that seemed to harm the poor and underserved, I could be heard saying of the initiator, "That person's crazy." My mother heard me say it so often that she said one day, "Jeffrey, you think everybody's crazy."

Now, the truth is, I don't think *everybody* is crazy. But, I admit that I do think a lot of people qualify. I have not yet gone, however, to the same degree as Presiding Bishop Charles Blake, pastor of West Angeles Church of God in Christ. When he was preaching in Indianapolis, he said that the way he is able to function in the midst of a dysfunctional world is to think of the world as an insane asylum where every person is a patient and he is on staff.

While I don't yet believe that *everybody* is crazy, I admit that I do use the word "crazy" a lot. I probably shouldn't use the word in my sermons because I am supposed to be preaching the *Good* News of Jesus Christ, and nobody wants to be called "crazy." But some of us *are* insane. There is no other explanation. That's what sin does. When we become addicted to sin, become in bondage to sin, that sin will make us crazy. Sin will cause us to hang out in places where we really don't want to be. Sin will have us hanging out with people we don't even like. Sin will have us drinking and taking drugs when we really don't want to be doing things like that. Sin will have us sleeping with people with whom we have no business sleeping. Sin will have us spending money we don't have. This happens because sin makes us insane.

Most of us have done something that we didn't want to do, we didn't plan to do, and we said we would never do. We even used to talk about people who did the very thing that we did. We would sometimes say, "Well, I've got issues, but I'm not as bad as they are. I would *never* do that." And then we found ourselves doing what we said we would never do. Then we looked in the mirror at ourselves and said, "I must have been crazy." Yes, we were, because sin makes us crazy.

That's why B.o.B, along with Nicki Minaj, sings, "Out of My Mind," a hip-hop tune that has lyrics referring to his brain leaving, being paranoid, and being messed up in other ways. I talked with you earlier about not listening to entertainers who curse, use the n-word, and disrespect themselves and others. It's interesting to me that these two hip hop artists who so freely do such things acknowledge that they are out of their minds. Maybe these two have come to a realization that can help them. You see, the first step in getting our minds right is to recognize when they aren't right. Son, what I don't want is for you to continue to do insane things. I don't want you to continue to act in crazy ways and yet think that you're okay. It isn't until you acknowledge the fact that you are out of your mind that you are finally in a position to get your mind right.

Step One: Get a Bible

So, how do we come to our senses? In order to come to our senses, we need to develop our sense of hearing. In Proverbs 4:20 (NLT) Solomon says, "My child, pay attention to what I say. Listen carefully to my words." We must pay attention to the Word of God. That causes me to ask you, son, "What have you been paying attention to? Who have you been listening to? Where do you get your theology? Where do you get your philosophy? Where do you get your mindset concerning life? Who have you been listening to?" It's important that I ask these questions because the reason some of us are insane is that we have not been paying attention to God's Word. When we get in the Word of God and get the wisdom of God—that is, both getting the knowledge from God and then applying it to our lives—we are able to get ourselves lined up with the will of God and the ways of God.

But if we don't get into the Word of God and are letting other voices influence us, it is no wonder that our lives are not going in the direction they are supposed to go. We cannot listen to a bunch of junk and think that our lives won't become junky. We can't listen to a bunch of mess and think that our lives won't be messy. We can't listen to a bunch of craziness and think we won't become crazy. Whatever we allow to get into our heads is eventually going to end up in our habits. That's why we have to get into God's Word and pay attention to what His Word says.

Son, I want you to get a Bible. You need to have a Bible of your own. I want you to open that Bible up every day and read from it. When you get into God's Word, it puts you in a position where you can begin to operate within the will of God. You need to get into the Word. Now, don't give me the argument, "I tried to get into the Bible, but when I tried to read it, I couldn't understand it." That's because you were reading Big Momma's King James Version. I want you to go to a bookstore and tell the salesperson, "I need to buy a Bible in everyday language I can understand." Get yourself a modern-day version, such as the New International Version, the New Living Translation, The Message, the Amplified Bible, or even the New King James Version. There are so many versions written in our present-day English language, not in the archaic English spoken by King James in the fifteenth century.

You need to understand that the King James Version was not the original version of the Bible. In fact, the original versions were not in English at all. Every translation, every version we have, including the King James, were all based on the original texts but then translated into a language that could be understood by people of a particular time period and language. Don't feel that you are being more spiritual or getting the "real Bible" if you read from the King James Version. I happen to love that version because of the poetic beauty of the language of that time. But more often I preach, teach, and study from a modern-day version because I preach to people in twenty-first-century America, not fifteenth-century England. So, ask a salesperson to show you a variety of modern translations, and then read a little bit from each of them until you find one that speaks to you—one that you can understand.

If we're going to get our mind right, we have to get into God's Word. That's important because when we know the Word of God and then hear people speak things that contradict that Word, we reject what they say immediately. But if we don't know what the Word says, we don't know what to accept or reject.

Recognizing His Voice

I was in Macon, Georgia, some time ago, preaching for a friend of mine who had just purchased a custom-made BMW convertible coupe. It was sweet. That was the first time I had ever ridden in a voice-activated car. The car was programmed to recognize my friend's voice. Whenever we got into the car, he would just speak to the car, and his voice activated the car. He would tell the car to start, and it started. He would tell the car to turn off, and it turned off. He would tell the car to access a particular radio station, and that station came on. He didn't have to touch a button or turn a key; he just spoke, and the car spoke back to him. As we were driving, the car would give him directions to the place we wanted to go.

After the service that night we got into the car and my friend remembered something he needed to get from the church; so he left me in the car and went back in. Now, I was sitting there in the car with nothing to do, so I started bossing his car around. I told the car to start, but it wouldn't start. I told the car to go to satellite radio, but it wouldn't change. I told the car what hotel I was staying in, but it wouldn't give me directions. After my futile attempts to get the car to do what I wanted, the car said to me, "Your voice is unrecognizable." The car wouldn't respond to me because it wasn't programmed to my voice. It was programmed for its owner's voice. When I tried to speak something into the car, it rejected me because I had an unrecognizable voice.

When you accepted Jesus as your personal Savior, you became His. You belong to Him. He bought you on a hill called Calvary. In verses 14 and 27 of John 10, Jesus said, "I am the good shepherd; I know my sheep and my sheep know me. . . .My sheep listen to my voice; I know them, and they follow me." So, when somebody says, "Let's go to the club," that voice is unrecognizable and the follower of Jesus doesn't listen to that strange voice. When a voice says, "Come sleep with me," the follower of Jesus doesn't yield to the temptation because he is led only by the voice of Jesus. If someone says, "Let's go get high," the Christian says, "I don't recognize that voice. I'm not going to follow it." When someone says, "You should drop out of school with me," that voice is unrecognizable and has no influence over the life of the follower of Christ. He has learned to listen to the voice of his Lord and Savior Jesus Christ, and he will not follow anyone else. If you are going to get your mind right, to come to your senses, you need to develop a good sense of hearing.

Envision His Vision

We not only need a good sense of hearing, but also good sight—that is, we need a clear sense of vision. Proverbs 3:21 (NLT) says, "My child, don't lose sight of common sense and discernment." This verse is basically saying, "Don't lose sight." We always need to keep common sense and discernment in sight. The wisdom of God and the Word of God will guide us, but we must keep our eyes upon them. How we see life will determine whether or not we keep within our right mind. Some of us are insane because of our world view—our vision, how we see life, our perceptions.

Proverbs 29:18 (KJV) says, "Where there is no vision, the people perish." If we are perishing, faltering, and failing, the Bible says that is because there is something wrong with how we see life. Some of us think we can see when we really can't see.

Once, that happened to me physically. Right now I can see fine because I wear contacts, and with my contacts in, I have better than 20/20 vision. But before I finally broke down and had my eyesight checked, I *thought* I was seeing, but I really wasn't. I assumed the blurriness and poor vision that was my experience was everyone's experience. When I was preaching from the pulpit, I could only see to the fourth row in the church. I didn't realize others could see to the back of the church. I thought my vision was "normal" and that everyone saw as I did. But I didn't realize that wasn't true until after I could see clearly. Then, I saw what I had been missing for years.

I recognized that, while I thought I had been seeing like everybody else, others were seeing farther and more clearly than I could.

My poor vision was brought to my attention when I was driving our guest pastor, Dr. Maurice Watson, around the city and I was looking for street signs. I was driving on I465 and I exited to get onto Shadeland. At one point, he asked me, "Man, can you see?" I guess I was squinting and didn't even realize it. I said, "Sure, I can see." He said, "No, you can't see." I insisted that I could, so he took his own glasses off, put them on my face, and for the first time, I could see. It was at that moment that I learned that all of those years, I hadn't been able to see clearly.

Some of us have such a distorted perception of life, but we think that's the way life really looks. It isn't until we enter into the light of Jesus Christ that we can finally see clearly. Once we come into the marvelous light of Jesus, it dawns on us that we haven't been seeing life clearly at all. The way we have seen life, isn't the way that everybody sees life.

Believe it or not, not everybody wakes up and fusses and cusses from the time they get up until the time they go to bed. Not everybody starts the day off with a drink. Not everybody is high by 11 a.m. Everybody doesn't put their wives down or beat their children. Not everybody drops out of school. Not everybody goes through life lazy and unable to keep a job. Not everybody is mean, evil, and hard to get along with. Not everybody wakes up in the morning thinking about whom they are going to manipulate today, of whom they are going to take advantage of today. If that's what life looks like to you, that's because you aren't seeing it clearly.

But when you get your heart right with Jesus, He helps you to see life in a way that you haven't been able to see before. Remember, you can't understand that you aren't seeing clearly until you do see clearly. That's why Solomon said, "My child, don't lose sight." And Solomon didn't want his son only to see *life* as God sees it, but he wanted him to see *himself* as God sees him. And God wants you to see *you* the way He sees you. Some of us are messed up because we don't see ourselves clearly. That means that we are not seeing ourselves the way God sees us.

Visualization Before Realization

Every now and then, God will show us something before He gives it to us. There is *visualization* before there is *realization*. We must be able to see ourselves as God sees us if we are ever going to *become* what God wants us to become. God shows it to us, and then He gives it to us. If God shows it to us, it means that we can have it, even if no one else sees it. If He shows us prosperity, or success, or greatness, we can see His vision realized in our lives, but that means that we must first see ourselves as God sees us.

Let me give you an example. RG3, Robert Griffin III, is a quarterback for the Washington Redskins and was the No. 2 pick for the 2012 NFL Draft. He had graduated from high school early, graduated from college early, and was a Heisman Trophy winner. During the first six games of the season, sportscasters said that he played better than anyone else in the NFL. He has everything going for him.

But his uncle tells a story about the time he went to sign RG3 up for football when he was about seven to nine years old. RG3's father was in the military, so he wrote home and asked the family to sign his son up for football. But when the uncle was on the way to sign his nephew up, he looked at how small and skinny he was, so he decided not to sign him up. He was afraid the other boys, bigger guys who were used to playing football in the inner city, would hurt him. He turned around and wouldn't sign him up. That's because when he saw RG3, he didn't see a football player. The next year, however, the boy's father was home. He took RG3 himself to sign him up to play. What the uncle couldn't see in him, his father could. And RG3 saw himself the way his father saw him. The uncle made this statement recently: "Here, I was driving with the future Heisman Trophy winner and didn't realize it. I was riding with the future Heisman Trophy winner and I turned around."

Son, not everyone will see in you what your heavenly Father sees in you. Someone driving with you along in his car may not realize that he is driving a future teacher, doctor, lawyer, president, or pastor. But that doesn't have to stop you from becoming whatever it is God has destined for your life. You just have to be sure, however, that you don't see yourself the way that person sees you. You have to see yourself the way your Father sees you.

There is *visualization* before there is *realization*. At this point you may only be able to visualize it, but if God lets you visualize it, He can enable you to realize it. Abraham was very old and his wife was past childbearing age when God gave them their son Isaac. After Abraham was obedient to God and willing to sacrifice that son back to God, God told Abraham that through Isaac He was going to give Abraham countless descendants and they would be a blessing to this world. God knew, however, that it was impossible for Abraham to grasp the magnitude of what He was telling him, so He gave him a visual to illustrate. He said to Abraham, "I will surely bless you and make your descendants as numerous as the stars in the sky and as the sand on the seashore. Your descendants will take possession of the cities of their enemies, and through your offspring all nations on earth will be blessed, because you have obeyed me" (Genesis 22:17-18). Abraham was then able to look up at the countless stars on any night, or look at the infinite grains of sand on the seashore, and rejoice in what God was going to do in his life.

In 2012 LeBron James won the MVP Award in the NBA Finals, and helped his team win the championship. But before the next season even started, LeBron James had already started visualizing winning it again. Visualization comes before realization. Tiger Woods sees himself winning a golf game before he ever tees off. When Michael Jordan was still playing with the Chicago Bulls, Coach Phil Jackson used to have the guys to lie down on the floor, close their eyes, and visualize winning. You have to visualize what you want before you can realize it. Son, if you can't see it before you see it, you're never going to see it. If God shows you something that He wants you to have, it doesn't matter if other folks can see it, but *you* need to see it, like God sees it.

Keep the Focus

Proverbs 4:25 says, "Let your eyes look straight ahead; fix your gaze directly before you." The writer is saying, "Keep your eyes on where you are going." It is a trick of the enemy to distract us. We may initially be able to see what God has for us. We may see his purpose for our lives, and we start heading towards it. But on the way, there are distractions. If we aren't careful, we'll take our eyes off the prize. We have to stay focused. We have to keep our eyes directed in the way we are headed.

My mentor, Dr. A. Louis Patterson, once asked me: "Do you know what it is that can keep you from getting what you want most?" I responded, "What is it that will prevent me from getting what I want most?" He replied, "What you want." He went on to explain that there is something I want *most*, but all of the other things that I want along the way will keep me from getting that one thing I want most. All of the other things I want are distractions.

The one thing I want most is to be a great preacher. Jesus forgave my sins, saved my soul, offered me another chance, and gave me this gift. What I want most is to use this gift He gave me, develop it, and become the best preacher I can possibly be for His sake and the sake of the kingdom. But do you know what will keep me from what I want most? Those things I just want some of.

Son, what is it that you want most? What is it that God has revealed to you? What have you been able to see — even if it was just a momentary glimpse? You have to stay focused and keep your eyes on that vision because this other little stuff that is not as important to you will keep you from what is most important.

Maybe you have a problem with this concept because, for whatever reason, you aren't able to see yourself successful at *anything*. Maybe you can't see yourself prosperous. Maybe you can't see yourself going to college. Maybe you can't see yourself in a healthy marital relationship. Maybe you can't see yourself being a good father. Why is that? It could be because you have never seen your vision modeled before you. Or, it could be because other people keep saying negative things to you that keep you feeling worthless and like a failure. That's why it is important to have Jesus Christ in your life. When Jesus saves you, the Holy Spirit comes to live within you and to help you to see things you couldn't see on your own.

There is a condition that can happen in the physical realm called macular degeneration. It is the loss of vision at the center of the retina. It causes blurred vision or a blind spot right in the center of one's vision. A person with macular degeneration can still see something, but can see nothing clearly when looking right at it. It affects reading, driving and even recognizing people on sight. A couple of years ago, however, someone invented a miniature telescope. It is so tiny, in fact, that it can be implanted in a person's eye and not even be noticed by most people looking at that individual. But the person with the telescope in their eye knows it is there because the things that for years had been blurry or indistinguishable come into focus again.

This illustrates what happens when we accept Jesus Christ as our Lord and Savior. God "implants" the Holy Spirit within us, so the things that we could not previously see clearly, we can see now. When Jesus says to us, as He did in John 15:3, "You are already clean because of the word I have spoken to you," we can see ourselves as clean inside—no longer tainted by the sins that we committed. And when God reveals to us His plan for us to be an educator, a doctor, a preacher, etc., we can see it because the Holy Spirit is revealing it to us. When God says we can become the fathers to our children that we never had, we can see that because the Holy Spirit reveals it to us. Whatever God envisions for us, we can see it now because the Holy Spirit is our spiritual telescope implanted within us to help us see things clearly—just as God sees them. Others may not be able to see the Holy Spirit, but we know He is within us. We know that because once we were blind, but now we can see!

Guard Your Heart

To get our minds right, we also need the sense of feeling—we need to be able to feel things with our hearts. There is power in emotion. Proverbs 4:23 says, "Above all else, guard your heart, for everything you do flows from it." Some of us have hard hearts. Sometimes we talk about other people being haters when we are haters ourselves. This happens when we don't guard our hearts. Jesus taught, "What goes into someone's mouth does not defile them, but what comes out of their mouth, that is what defiles them" (Matthew 15:11). When Peter couldn't understand what He meant, He explained, "Don't you see that whatever enters the mouth goes into the stomach and then out of the body? But the things that come out of a person's mouth come from the heart, and these defile them. For out of the heart come evil thoughts—murder, adultery, sexual immorality, theft, false testimony, slander" (Matthew 15:17-19).

Some of us have such hard hearts that nothing touches us—nothing. We can hear about someone being sick, some young woman being raped, or some child being abused, but it doesn't touch us. There is no sense of feeling. Nothing gets to us. We lose the power of emotion. That's why the Lord tells us to guard our hearts. It's from our hearts that our passion and our compassion come. That is where our freedom comes. That is where our success comes. That is where the realization of our visualizations comes.

When we have a sense of passion, it has to be about someone other than ourselves. In Mark 12:30 Jesus said that the greatest commandment is this: "Love the Lord your God with all your heart and with all your soul and with all your mind and with all your strength." Notice that the word "all" is repeated four times in that sentence. That repetition means that Jesus was emphasizing that we are to put EVERYTHING into loving God—*all* of our heart, *all* of our soul, *all* of our mind, and *all* of our strength. That is passion. We can't say we are passionate about something if we are giving it less than our all.

If we are loving God with our *all*, nobody will have to compel us to go to church, to pray, to get into the Bible, to tithe, or to serve God. We will do all of these things because we are passionate about God. We will *want* to worship God, to please Him, and to show Him that we love Him.

And when we love God with our *all*, that love will reach out to others, too. Right after saying that the greatest commandment was to love God, Jesus said the second commandment is to "love your neighbor as yourself" (Mark 12:31). How do you *feel* about other people? There is power in emotion. In fact, 1 John 4:20 says, "Whoever claims to love God yet hates a brother or sister is a liar. For whoever does not love their brother and sister, whom they have seen, cannot love God, whom they have not seen." And Jesus said in John 13:35, "By this everyone will know that you are my disciples, if you love one another." The evidence of our relationship with Jesus is our love for one another. Some of us may speak in other tongues, preach a great sermon, or hold all sorts of positions in the church, but if we don't love others, we cannot call ourselves disciples of Jesus.

Let me offer you a definition of "love." Love is an evaluating of another person's needs and doing what we need to do to meet those needs in a spirit of self-sacrifice even when we don't feel like doing it. That's love. Jesus told us to love our neighbors as ourselves. That means that we will take care of our neighbors' needs as we would our own. We will seek our neighbors' best interests even as we would our own. We will want our neighbors to have a relationship with God through Jesus Christ even as we have for ourselves. We want them to have a quality education, a good marriage, healthy children, and a rewarding job—all the same things we want for ourselves. Insanity begins to set in when we are focused totally inward on ourselves and don't care about anyone else.

Let me ask you about someone it should be natural for you to love. When did you last show your wife that you love her? When did you last evaluate her needs in a spirit of self-sacrifice, even when you didn't feel like doing it? And what about your mother? When did you last let her know that you love her? And what about your friends? When did you last evaluate their needs and try to meet them? Until you get to the point that you give sacrificially of yourself and all that you have, you really won't understand the power of emotion, the power of passion.

It Takes Passion

You also have to be passionate about God's destiny for your life. The Bible speaks many times against laziness. It is a sin that can rob you of what God has for you. Laziness is an insidious practice because it can slip up on you. For instance, how many hours in a day can you sit and play an electronic game? Set it aside and go out and throw a *real* football for a while, or go out and play a *real* game of basketball. Maybe watching TV is your thing. Why do you spend every night *watching* someone else experiencing life instead of experiencing life for yourself? Turn it off! Or maybe you are content just to eat and sleep. You don't really *do* much of anything. That's sad. God has so much more in store for you than that!

What is it that you're passionate about? What is it that you go after? What are you trying to do? There is power in passion. Until you show passion about something, you won't experience the power that accompanies it. You will also find that people with passion can't identify with those without passion, and people without passion can't identify with those with passion. People with a work ethic cannot identify with people who won't work. And people who won't work can't identify with people with a work ethic. They ask, "Are you going to work *again*?" "Yes, I do it every day, at least five days a week."

Perhaps you do have passion. Maybe, like I've talked with you about before, you are one of those who want to be a gangster rapper or an NBA basketball player. But son, passion has to be directed towards reality, not fantasy. It's one thing to have a great imagination. It's another thing altogether to live in a fantasy world where we never accomplish anything because we're always waiting for our big break, waiting for our ship to come in, or waiting to be discovered. Some people never do anything in their entire lives because they are waiting for the fantasy. That's foolishness.

The Book of Proverbs talks a lot about choosing wisdom over foolishness. There are some things that, as Christians, we can automatically rule out as a career choice. For instance, there is no way I could ever be a gangsta' rapper because I can't swear or cuss people out as a follower of Jesus. And I don't demean women, disrespect authority, or behave violently towards others. I live in a different kingdom from those who do such things. I have a different world view.

Let's say that you are one of those who want to be in the NBA. You don't mind if you're not a starting player. You don't mind being that twelfth man on the bench. You would be content just to be part of the team so that you can brag to your friends that you made it. Well, let me ask you this: If that's what you really want, are you making a thousand jump shots a day? Are you getting up early and going to the gym for a couple hours before school every day to practice lay-ups? Are you heading to the basketball court each day after school to play? If you've already made your high school team, are you giving it your best, following your team's rules, and doing all you can to improve? Are you also keeping up with your homework and making good grades so that you can get a scholarship to make it on a good college team? Also, son, face reality. How tall are you? The average NBA player is six foot eight—and those are the guards! Are you passionate about a reality, or a fantasy?

Save Fantasyland for Disney World

I graduated from Arlington High School when Mr. Robert Turner was the principal. I still like to go back to the school, walk around, and talk with some of the boys there because I want them to see a man who graduated from Arlington and made it. Then they can say, "Well, if he made it from here, I can make it, too. If he did okay, then I have a chance, too." On one of my visits, then principal Dr. Jacqueline Greenwood asked me if I could go into detention and talk to the young people there. In all honesty, I didn't want to go because I did my time in detention while I was a student at Arlington, and that was enough for me. But out of respect for Dr. Greenwood, I agreed to do it.

About twenty or twenty-five young people were in detention that day. I wasn't sure what I was going to say, but I started my talk by asking, "What do you want to be? What are your career goals?" My point was to let them know that, whatever they wanted to be, they couldn't get there if they spent a lot of time in detention. Detention is not on the road to success.

Sadly, there was a young man in that group, a five-foot-four sophomore, who said in all seriousness that he was going to play in the NBA. I asked him, "Did you make your high school team?"

"No, I didn't make it."

"Why do you think you can make it in the NBA if you couldn't make it at Arlington High School?"

"Well, the coaches here are stupid. They don't know what they're doing."

"So, is it the coach's fault that you didn't make the team? Is it the coach's fault that you're in detention? Son, if you're going to make it in the NBA, you have to be not only the best player in your school, but you have to be one of the best players in the state! Remember, there are only four hundred and fifty players in the NBA. They have no mediocre players. In fact, a 'mediocre' player in the NBA is still one of the best players in the world. He may not be a Kobe Bryant or LeBron James, but he is still better than almost any man who is *not* in the NBA. And he has the work ethic to keep his position there. He isn't goofing off like someone who ends up in detention. He's a professional with the self-discipline to keep doing what he needs to do to keep getting better at his game. And son, don't forget about your height. At five foot four, you really don't have much of a chance. And don't bring up Muggsy Bogues. There was only one Muggsy Bogues, and you're not him! And you're not Earl Boykins either! Son, face reality!"

His Ways Are Higher Than Our Ways

Just because you are passionate for the game doesn't mean that God wants you to be an NBA player. Cast your vision wider. The NBA is a multibillion dollar industry. It takes a lot more than the players to operate a business of that size. They have coaches, assistant coaches, scouts, statisticians, broadcasters, writers, marketing and PR people, managers, senior executives, vice presidents—and many, many others. Just because you have a passion for the game doesn't mean you will be one of the four hundred and fifty players. If you have such a great passion for the game, look for a position for which your gifts and abilities match the job description.

I had a passion for basketball when I was at Arlington, and I still love it. But I never got to be a player in the game. Yet I did get to be a pray-er for those in the game! I was a chaplain for the Indiana Pacers and got the opportunity to share the gospel of Jesus Christ with every single team in the NBA League. God said, "I didn't give you the passion so that you could be a *player*; I gave you the passion so that you could be a *pray-er*. I want you to make a difference in the players' lives."

Distractions Cause Crashes

Son, not only do you have to be realistic in terms of your passion, but you also have to be selective. Think about David. Why was he walking around on his roof that day anyhow? Was he just being lazy? Didn't he have something better to do since he was the king? As it happens, he should have been leading his armies into battle that day, but he didn't go! Kings were supposed to be at the forefront of the battle. They were supposed to be the leaders. But David chose not to on that day. He decided to take a day off. He just wanted to chill. He had no passion for his work. So while he was not doing what he should have been doing, along came a distraction.

He looked out from his rooftop and saw a fine, dark-skinned woman who was naked because she was bathing. It would be hard to find fault with David for being distracted by a beautiful naked woman he just happened to see. But then he inquired about her and learned that she was Bathsheba, Uriah's wife. It was at that point he made the wrong choice. Instead of diverting his attention and recognizing that she was off-limits, he had her brought to his palace where he slept with her, and later he sent her back home. A couple months later he got word that she was pregnant with his child.

Then David began sinning even more in an effort to cover up his sin of adultery. He didn't guard his heart, so he was sleeping with someone he shouldn't have been sleeping with in the first place. He didn't guard his heart, so he usurped the authority of his position. He didn't guard his heart, so now he was involved in a conspiracy to commit murder. After he sinned, instead of 'fessing up, he tried to cover it up, and his life ended up being jacked up.

Finally, a true friend went to David and told him that God saw everything he had done, so he needed to confess his sin to Him. When David repented, there were still repercussions from his sin, but his heart was turned to God, who ministered to him and helped him turn his life back around. That's what we all have to do, son. We need to confess our sins and repent of our wrong choices, as well as our failure to guard our hearts. When we do that, we begin to come back into our right minds.

The Power of Communication

Proverbs 4:24 says, "Keep your mouth free of perversity; keep corrupt talk far from your lips." That means that we are supposed to engage in honest, positive conversation. When you speak, what do you say? We need to make sure that we are not cussing, lying, spreading rumors, being negative, and criticizing. We have to understand the power of communication. In the New King James Version, Romans 10:17 reads, "So then faith comes by hearing, and hearing by the word of God." When we open the Bible and read it, we take the Word of God into our heads and we begin to see ourselves the way God sees us. Then we need to speak what we hear God saying. We need to say the same things about our lives that God is saying through His Word. There is power in speech. There is power in the words we say. In Romans 4:17 Paul speaks of "the God who . . . calls into being things that were not." God can speak things into existence. We need to tap into that power as well. We need to think as God thinks and speak as God speaks. God doesn't look at what is and think, *Well, that's a shame, but that's the way it is*. No! God sees what can be. And He speaks into existence what can be.

We need to follow God's example. We need to speak into our lives those things that God has promised. We need to say: "I will overcome my enemies," "I will prosper," "I will have my needs met," "I will love my wife," and "I will take care of my children" because "I can do all this through him who gives me strength" (Philippians 4:13).

God will say only what is true. If we say what He says, we are speaking what can only be true. Keep in mind that the person we hear speak the most is ourselves. So, we must speak positive, loving, affirmative thoughts to ourselves.

Welcome Home

Even when we feel that we have lost our minds, it is still possible to change and recover. Remember, I shared with you in an earlier chapter about the young man who demanded to have his inheritance even while his father was still alive. He took his father's money, disrespected his father, left his father's home, and squandered all that his father gave him. He spent money, spent money, spent money, and kept on spending money— until it was all gone. All of the people who hung out with him when he had money to spend now left him. He was broke, homeless, unemployed, and possessed absolutely nothing. He took a job, but the job that he took contradicted his convictions about God. He had said he would never do something like this, but here he was, a hired servant, feeding pigs that, to a Jew, were unclean animals. He was fattening pigs for others to eat, when he himself considered eating that animal a sin. He had reached bottom.

Luke 15:17 says, "When he came to his senses, he said, 'How many of my father's hired servants have food to spare, and here I am starving to death!'" The prodigal son knew that his only hope was in his father, so he went home. He told his father that he didn't even have to treat him as a son, and begged his father to let him return as a servant. But his father welcomed him home with loving arms. The father hugged him and kissed him. He put a ring on his finger to remind him that he was still his son. He got him cleaned up, put clean clothes on him, and threw a big welcome home party for him. The father said, "For this son of mine was dead and is alive again; he was lost and is found" (Luke 15:24). Jesus told that story because the father in the parable illustrates the attitude of our heavenly Father toward us.

Romans 3:23 says that "all have sinned and fall short of the glory of God." We have all strayed away at some point—refusing to open ourselves to the Word of God, refusing to obey God, and refusing to follow the advice of those who are wise, of those who love us. We have done what we wanted to do and no one could stop us. We keep on and on in our sin until we lose everything—our self-respect, our health, our money, our dreams for the future, our clear conscience,

169

our relationships, our sanity, and even ourselves. We find ourselves doing things we said we would never do, and we do those things that contradict our Christian beliefs. One day, we look around and realize that we are living with pigs.

It's time then for us to come to our senses. It is time to come home. And when we do, God is just like the father in that story. He embraces us, forgives us, reminds us that we are still His children, and lets us know that He still loves us. Then God and all of heaven celebrate because the one who was dead is alive again, and the one who was lost is now found. Son, never be afraid to come home.

An Example to Consider: Legion

Please take out your Bible and read Mark 5:1-18.

If there was ever a man with an identity problem, it was Legion. He was filled with many evil spirits, so he did not even speak in terms of "I," but of "we." He was not the man he was born to be because the evil within him had control over his life. Instead of walking among the living, Legion hung out with the dead among the tombs. Instead of doing those things that were healthy and good for him, he engaged in self-destructive habits. Mark 5:5 says, "Night and day among the tombs and in the hills he would cry out and cut himself with stones."

But one day, Jesus came in a boat to the place where Legion lived. The first words from the mouth of this deranged man were, "What do you want with me, Jesus, Son of the Most High God?" (Mark 5:7). And the second sentence, (from the same verse), was truly ironic. He said, "In God's name, don't torture me!" Only an insane man would invoke the name of God in an effort to tell the Son of God what not to do. But Jesus looked past all of the demons inside of Legion and saw the man himself. He delivered Legion by commanding the spirits within him to depart from him. Of the townspeople Mark 5:15 says, "When they came to Jesus, they saw the man who had been possessed by the legion of demons, sitting there, dressed and in his right mind."

171

Notice that before Jesus came, people saw "Legion"—the evil resident within this body—but now "they saw the man." This man got his life back. He experienced a physical change in that he was now clothed. He experienced a psychological change: he was in his right mind. And he experienced a spiritual change: he was sitting at the feet of Jesus. *That* is transformation. *That* is what God can do for us. It doesn't matter how crazy we are because of the evil within us. God can deliver us and bring about physical, mental, emotional, and spiritual changes in our lives. He is able to get us in our right minds.

Dear God,

At times, it seems that we are not experiencing all that You have for us. Evil, in its various forms, resides in our bodies, minds, and spirits. At first we thought we could control how much we sinned and stop at any time; but now, it's so strong, we can't break away—no matter how hard we try. Therefore, we need You, Jesus, to come to us. We need You to deliver us from evil and clothe us in our right minds so that we might serve You. Amen.

CHAPTER 5

Enough of No Love

Drink water from your own well—

    share your love only with your wife.

Why spill the water of your springs in the streets,

    having sex with just anyone?

You should reserve it for yourselves.

    Never share it with strangers.

Let your wife be a fountain of blessing for you.

    Rejoice in the wife of your youth.

She is a loving deer, a graceful doe.

    Let her breasts satisfy you always.

    May you always be captivated by her love.

Why be captivated, my son, by an immoral woman,

    or fondle the breasts of a promiscuous woman?

For the LORD sees clearly what a man does,

    examining every path he takes.

An evil man is held captive by his own sins;

    they are ropes that catch and hold him.

He will die for lack of self-control;

    he will be lost because of his great foolishness.

(Proverbs 5:15-23 NLT)

Wrong Can't Be Right

S on, let me tell you about a young man named Amnon, who allowed himself to fall in love with a beautiful woman named Tamar. He should never have let his thoughts about her develop because Tamar was his half-sister. Tamar was a virgin who was keeping herself pure for her future husband. She was certainly not interested in a romantic relationship with her half-brother. The Law God gave to Moses forbade marriage between brothers and sisters. (See Leviticus 18:9.)

But Amnon took advice from the wrong person. He confided his passionate affection for Tamar in his friend Jonadab, who was also his cousin. The Bible says that Jonadab was "crafty." (See 2 Samuel 13 to read this story.) Now, Amnon should not have been listening to such a person, but he wanted Tamar and was willing to listen to anybody who would help him to get what he wanted. Following Jonadab's advice, Amnon pretended to be sick. When King David, his father, came to see him, Amnon asked him to send Tamar to prepare a meal and feed him because he was feeling so poorly. Without even imagining that Amnon had any ulterior motives, David did as he requested.

Crossing the Line

When Tamar came, she prepared the meal in front of Amnon, who was lying down, and those who were with him. When the food was ready, she set a tray before him, but he told everyone else to leave and then he told Tamar to bring him his food in his bedroom and feed it to him there. Willing to care for her sick brother, she took the food into his bedroom and began feeding him. Suddenly, Amnon grabbed her and told her to come to bed with him.

She protested, but he raped her. She had cried out to him, "No, my brother! . . . . Don't force me! Such a thing should not be done in Israel! Don't do this wicked thing" (2 Samuel 13:12). But he paid no attention to her "no." He paid no attention to her protests. He paid no attention to the reminder that God would see this as a "wicked thing." Amnon cared only about satisfying his lust, so despite the cries of his sister, he raped her.

Son, anytime a woman says "no" in a sexual encounter, that's when the activity stops. Nothing else matters. Her "no" brings everything to a screeching halt. It doesn't matter what led up to that moment. It doesn't matter where you took her for dinner. It doesn't matter how many trips you've taken together. It doesn't matter what you've done together in the past. It doesn't matter what you thought she was saying. When she says "no," you stop. Anytime you go beyond a woman's "no," you are guilty of sexually assaulting her. Of course, we know that sex outside of marriage is a sin, so we should never put ourselves in a situation anyhow in which we are making sexual advances to anyone to whom we are not married.

Lust Destroys

Amnon lusted after Tamar and was not content until he had her. But as soon as he got what he thought he wanted, he no longer wanted her. In fact, his so-called "love" turned to hatred. Listen to the plight of Tamar in verses 15 through 19:

> Then Amnon hated her with intense hatred. In fact, he hated her more than he had loved her. Amnon said to her, "Get up and get out!"

> "No!" she said to him. "Sending me away would be a greater wrong than what you have already done to me."

> But he refused to listen to her. He called his personal servant and said, "Get this woman out of my sight and bolt the door after her." So his servant put her out and bolted the door after her. She was wearing an ornate

robe, for this was the kind of garment the virgin daughters of the king wore. Tamar put ashes on her head and tore the ornate robe she was wearing. She put her hands on her head and went away, weeping aloud as she went.

And, as has often been the situation when a woman reveals that she has been raped, even her own brother responded, "Be quiet for now, my sister; he is your brother. Don't take this thing to heart" (2 Samuel 13:20). He silences her. He tells her not to let it get to her. He doesn't bring this awful crime to light. He doesn't see that Amnon is dealt with by the proper authorities. He doesn't stand up for his sister when she needs him most. He lets her carry the burden of the shame and the memories of the violence done to her. That same verse then continues, "And Tamar lived in her brother Absalom's house, a desolate woman." Yet, while Absalom did nothing to comfort or vindicate his sister after the rape, he never forgot what Amnon had done. Two years later, Amnon paid with his life for what he had done against Tamar when Absalom ordered his servants to kill him.

Love or Lust: What's the Difference?

Think about this peculiar situation. Amnon had said he was in love. But a man doesn't violate a woman he loves. He doesn't hurt a woman he loves. He doesn't pretend to be something he is not before the woman he loves. He doesn't force her to do something she does not want to do. I think Amnon exemplified something that still holds true today—too many people mistake lust for love. Being sexually stimulated by a woman does not mean the same thing as being in love with her.

There are distinct differences between love and lust. Love is self*less*; lust is self*ish*. Love looks out for the other person; lust looks out for itself. Love seeks the best good and looks for ways to meet the needs of the person who is loved; lust seeks satisfaction of its own desires, its own will and its own way. The enemy uses our own lust against us.

James 1:13-14 says, "When tempted, no one should say, 'God is tempting me.' For God cannot be tempted by evil, nor does he tempt anyone; but each person is tempted when they are dragged away by their own evil desire and enticed." The apostle James goes on to say in verse 15, "Then, after desire has conceived, it gives birth to sin; and sin, when it is full-grown, gives birth to death." So, our lusts lead us to sin, and then our sin leads us to death. Our spiritual enemy uses our own lusts to bring us down. He uses our own sinful desires to lead us into sin. He uses our willingness to go against God, the will of God, and the nature of God to bring about our downfall.

Son, you need to be able to recognize genuine love. Too many people go all of their lives without ever experiencing true love. I feel sorry for them. For a man to go his whole life without ever properly loving or receiving love from a woman is a very sad thing. People who go from one lustful relationship to another never know what they are missing. Some men believe that the more relationships they have, the more they are proving their manhood. Son, dogs do that. Dogs go from one female to another. That doesn't make them a man.

Tame the Fantasy

We can never love a woman properly until we see a woman properly. We can never love her the way we are supposed to love her until we *see* her the way we are supposed to see her. If we objectify a woman, we cannot love her. When we treat her like an object rather than a subject, like an *it* rather than a *thou*, like a thing rather than a person, we cannot have genuine love for her.

For most of us men living in America, our image of womanhood has been distorted. Our image is dysfunctional. That's because some men get their image of womanhood from gangsta' rap, which refers to women by the b-word or the h-word. Some men also get their erroneous images from their peers who speak of women as sexual objects and demean them in their everyday conversation. Some men get their images from movies and television, where most of the sexual situations portrayed involve fornication or adultery. Very seldom do we see a husband and a wife engaging in warm, loving, sexual situations. Some men get their warped images of women from pornography. I've read that 70 percent of young men from eighteen to twenty-four view pornography at least once a month.

And, just watching celebrities in television and the movies gives us the idea that women should be perfect in face and form.

A real woman hardly stands a chance when so many men are comparing her to the false image of women that they have hidden in their hearts. If a woman has a healthy self-esteem and expects a man to respect her, some men will accuse her of being uppity and unapproachable. If a woman doesn't respond as a sexual object, feeding some ineffectual man's low self-esteem by letting him grope her body, such a man will say she is cold. If a woman isn't willing to operate in the same way as a porn star, some men may actually think there is something wrong with *her*. If a woman doesn't look like Halle Berry or Beyoncé, she doesn't measure up to the image of some men's fantasies; therefore, to them she isn't worth getting to know. Instead of accepting each woman as a whole person, created by God and created in the image of God, some men will usurp the authority of God and try to re-create her into some image they have fixed in their minds, which is dysfunctional.

In the Image of God

When God created the first woman, He did not ask a man for suggestions. God first made Adam. Then, when He was ready to make a woman, He put Adam to sleep and took out one of his ribs. He didn't wake Adam up until the woman's creation was complete. He didn't want Adam to be involved in the making of a woman because he could not have the right image of a woman. The only females Adam had seen up to that point were lions and tigers and bears (oh, my!). God determined that He was not going to let Adam's image of a female influence His creation of a woman. God had already decided that He was going to create woman after His own image, just as He had made man. When we cannot accept and appreciate a woman—especially our wife—as she is, we're actually saying that God didn't know what He was doing. If we refuse to see God in her and value the person she is, we'll just want to re-create her into the image of *woman* that we have conjured up in our own minds, under the influence of the popular media of today. If we do that, we'll never get around to understanding what real love is.

How tragic to go through life without ever experiencing genuine love. Real love is a safe haven in which we can be totally ourselves and accepted unconditionally. Real love brings intimacy and ecstasy. In his poem, "In Memoriam," Alfred Lord Tennyson wrote:

'Tis better to have loved and lost
Than never to have loved at all.

Humankind was created for love, which includes both the love of God and love of one another. In fact, the Bible likens the marriage relationship to the relationship between God and His people. For a man to cut himself off from the possibility of such an intimate relationship because of a false image that he carries in his mind,

181

or a lustful image he carries in his heart, is to keep himself from being fully human and to keep himself from better understanding the Divine.

True Love Begins with You

If you are going to enter into a healthy relationship and experience true love, it starts with you, son. That's why Solomon begins Proverbs 5 by saying, "My son, pay attention to my wisdom; listen carefully to my wise counsel" (v. 1 NLT). What we fill our head with and what we fill our heart with determines our destiny. You could choose the most loving, caring, Christian woman in the world, but if your head isn't right, you're going to mess it up. A good relationship starts with you.

So, son, I want to ask you a few questions. What have you been filling your head with? What have you been watching? What have you been reading? What have you been downloading? What you are putting into your head is going to make a difference in whether you experience a loving, fulfilling relationship.

Let me offer you an illustration. In the sports world right now, there is an increased focus on the long-term effects of concussions. This is the case not just in football, but in other sports as well—and it doesn't just occur in pro ball, but also in college, high school, and younger age groups. To try to help detour those negative consequences, a company has come out with a padding intended to be worn on the outside of a helmet or cap. When the player's head is wrapped securely in this cushioning material, the player will be protected from the likelihood of a serious concussion.

Naturally, parents, coaches, players, and the manufacturing company are happy about this development. I've read, however, that scientists are not sharing their joy. Scientists are saying that it isn't what is on the outside of the helmet that will make a difference, but rather what is on the inside. They say that it doesn't matter how thick the padding is outside, if there is no protection on the inside, there is still a risk of injury.

What I am trying to say to you, son, is that it isn't what is outside your brain that will make a difference, but what is on the inside. Gangsta rap isn't going anywhere. Pornography isn't going anywhere. Movies and television aren't going anywhere. These are multibillion dollar industries. They aren't suddenly going to fall away. All of these things, and probably new ones along the way, will serve to threaten our well-being and our destiny. But these things will not have a determining effect on us if we have the Word of God on the inside of our brains. If we are focusing on our relationship with God and getting into His Word on a daily basis, we will walk in His ways and find safety in His presence. The wisdom, principles, and mind of God active on the inside will protect us from all the negative stuff we will encounter on the outside.

God's Order of Things

When you read Proverbs 5, you'll see that it flows from "head" to "wed" to "bed." Let me show you what I mean. The very beginning of that chapter talks about wisdom, wise counsel, and discernment—those things that relate to the head. Then, after a warning about not giving in to the temptation of immorality, verse 15 instructs us to "share your love only with your wife," and follows up with counsel that relates to being wed. Then it speaks in very explicit terms about what happens in the bed. For instance, it says that, as a man, you should not "spill the water of your springs in the street." That is, your sexual release should happen only with your wife in your own bed, not with any other woman you find in the streets. Verse 19 speaks about fondling the breasts of your own wife and being satisfied with her, not seeking sexual gratification from some other woman besides your own wife. So this chapter has a message for us about using our head, honoring the one to whom we're wed, and enjoying sexual satisfaction with that person in our bed.

Sadly, too many of us want to ignore the head, skip the wed, and jump right into bed. Then we wonder why our lives are so dysfunctional. If you don't use your head, you might be picking up a stalker along the way. You also might be choosing some woman who has no capacity to love you, but instead is totally focused on herself and what pleases her. Or, you might end up with someone who satisfies your immediate lust but can't begin to satisfy your deeper desire for a lifelong love. By the time you've played around for a while, your life will be messed up. You can be on your way up, but if you attach yourself to a lowdown woman, you'll find yourself spiraling downward.

Beauty or Beast?

That's why, in Proverbs 5:3-9, Solomon tells his sons what type of woman to avoid. Beginning with verse 15, he talks about what a relationship should be like between a man and the right woman. Solomon wants his sons to see the contrast between the woman they are supposed to seek after and the woman from whom they are warned to flee. Solomon uses this chapter to teach his sons what to look for in a wife and instruct them about those principles that will create a happy marriage to last a lifetime.

God did a similar thing with Adam. The first man was surrounded by animals, but there was no partner for him because no one like him existed. He didn't have anyone with whom he could share intimately or love as he loved God. Genesis 2:18 says, "The Lord God said, 'It is not good for the man to be alone. I will make a helper suitable for him.'" God wasn't going to give Adam just *any* helper, but a "helper suitable for him." God created Adam. He knew him intimately and understood his deepest needs. Not just any helper would do for him. God knew that if his mate didn't fit (if she was not compatible), his marriage wasn't going to be able to function. So He created a woman especially for Adam.

But God didn't create Eve immediately. He first caused other beasts to pass before Adam and whatever Adam called them, that's what they were. It wasn't until later on that God created a helper fit, or suitable, for Adam. By letting all these animals pass before him first, Adam got the opportunity to see all of the beasts that were not suitable to be his partner so that when his bride came along, he would see the difference and appreciate her.

One of the reasons why I appreciate my wife so very much and why we have been married for twenty-six years is that before God brought her along, I met a lot of beasts along the way. By encountering so many of them, I eventually realized what I did not want in my life; so I kept watching and waiting, knowing that my bride would be different from all of them. I may have had a variety of names for all of those women, but only when I met Lady Sharon could I say, "She is bone of my bone and flesh of my flesh."

Fooled by Sweetness

Sometimes men are fooled by what they encounter along the way to meeting their brides. That's understandable when you look at the description of what a man would see initially. Proverbs 5:3 says, "For the lips of an immoral woman are as sweet as honey, and her mouth is smoother than oil." She's a smooth talker with a lot of experience with men, so she knows what they want to hear. She knows how to attract a man. It's easy to be tempted by such a woman because she seems so sweet and smooth. But son, all of them start off sweet and smooth. That's why you can't rush into a relationship. You can't just go by the initial sweetness and smoothness.

This is one of the reasons I have reservations about online dating. Yes, I admit that I am fifty years old and this is a different day from when my wife and I met. However, I still have trouble believing that you will get to know the real person by what you read online. People can write anything about themselves and sound sweet and smooth. But it isn't until later on that you would discover whether or not all that you read is true. In this day and age, people can also alter photos to make themselves look quite different from their real appearance.

Again, before things go too far, you need to get to know this person offline. Sadly, some men are interested only in a woman's description. They want to see a picture and to know her measurements. But they ought to be checking out her IQ as well as her physical dimensions. If she has a banging body but a messed-up brain, that's not going to be a good match for you.

You need to also look at her spiritual life. She may be sweet, but does she have salvation? She may be fine, but does she have faith? She's cute, but does she have character? She's pretty, but does she live by the principles of God? You need to slow things down, son. You need to take time to get to know the person behind the pretty face. You need to get to know how she treats other people. You need to know if she has a healthy, growing relationship with God. You need to know if she shares your values and wants what you want in life. You need to know far more than simply what is apparent on the outside or sweet to your ears.

You don't want to look only at her description; you also need to know the direction she is going in life. Look again at the verses we're focusing on in this chapter. Proverbs 5:3-6 (NLT) says,

> For the lips of an immoral woman are as sweet as honey, and her mouth is smoother than oil. But in the end she is as bitter as poison, as dangerous as a double-edged sword. Her feet go down to death; her steps lead straight to the grave. For she cares nothing about the path to life. She staggers down a crooked trail and doesn't realize it.

Yes, "her lips are as sweet as honey and her mouth is smoother than oil," but "her feet go down to death; her steps lead straight to the grave." If you follow after her, that's the direction you will be headed as well. In the King James Version, verse 5 reads, "Her feet go down to death; her steps take hold on hell." In a way, that's a more apt description because hell isn't just a destination, and it isn't always experienced only in the afterlife. Many men live in a hell of their own making even today. They may appear to have it all together, but if you were an invisible guest in their homes, you would realize that they have a hell of a life with their spouses. The women who seemed so sweet and lured them quickly into marriage are now making their lives miserable. Why? Because "she cares nothing about the path to life."

Going My Way?

Son, before you become serious about a woman, you need to know the direction she is headed. You need to know if she will bring you life or bring you death. You need to know if she will offer you a taste of heaven or the bitter foretaste of hell.

Imagine that you're standing in front of an elevator. If you are on the fourth floor and you want to go up to the fortieth floor, you don't just rush in when the elevator opens. No, you stop and look up at the signs to see if it's going up or down. If it's going down, it isn't your ride. You are on your way up.

Let's suppose that you get out of school and go to your school bus to get home. You don't just jump on the first bus you see. Twenty or thirty buses may be sitting there, but only one will go the direction you are going. Only one will take you to your desired destination. So, you look carefully at the signs on the buses to determine which one is yours.

Recently I was riding in a plane coming back from Atlanta. While I was sitting in my seat, a flight attendant said over the intercom, "If Indianapolis is not your destination, you need to deplane right now."

All of the planes in that area of the airport were owned by the same company and they all looked alike. But only one of them was going to my destination.

Son, what I'm trying to tell you is that not all women will be going to the same destination as you. You are a child of God. You have a destiny to fulfill in this lifetime, and you have a home in heaven where you will spend eternity. You are not headed towards a meaningless life without purpose or goals. You are not headed towards hell, and you surely don't want to be attached to a spouse who will make you feel as though you are there already. You need to look at the signs before you commit to a woman. You need to know not only what she says, but to be able to see the direction she is taking. Who's driving her bus? If it isn't Jesus, the two of you will be in constant turmoil, trying to drag the other person in a direction that you or she isn't going.

Slow Down!

The major thing to keep in mind as you are developing a new relationship is that you need to slow down. You start as friends, then you begin dating, then you become engaged, and then you get married. Marriage isn't just about the bed. Don't try to hurry through the process of getting to know her just because you want to get her in bed. Some men jump into the bed too soon. Some even get married too soon.

You need to *slow down*. Son, God is not trying to keep you from having sex. He originated sex. He made it pleasurable. He wants you to enjoy it. What kind of God would have created something so amazing, so fulfilling, and so fun and then say, "But you can't have any"? What kind of God would do that? Certainly not our God. God isn't trying to keep you from having sex. He's just trying to keep you from killing yourself while you are having sex.

When we built the first of our church's three locations, one of the things we most appreciated was having a parking lot of our own. We hadn't had that previously. Our former church building had been located in an inner-city area; so we just had to park on the street, along with all of the neighbors who lived there—which became more and more problematic for them as our numbers increased. One of the reasons we had to leave the area was that not only had we outgrown the sanctuary, but we had no place for people to park. So at our new location, we had acres of parking available.

We encountered a problem, though. The parking lot was brand new, so it was nice and smooth. Unfortunately, some people were driving fast onto the parking lot, having no regard for the people who were walking through it. This was especially challenging because we had a school back then, along with a daycare center, and people were coming and going throughout every day. So, after we moved into the building, we felt the need to put in speed bumps to slow people down. We didn't install the speed bumps to keep people from coming in. We installed the speed bumps so that people would slow down and come in safely.

In the same way, God is not trying to keep you from having sex. He isn't trying to keep you from coming into a marriage relationship. He's just trying to slow you down, so that you can enter in safely.

Remember also that verse 15 says, "Drink water from your own cistern, running water from your own well." You are to have sex only with your own wife. So many brothers have totally messed up their lives, as well as the lives of others, because they tried to have more than one woman.

Keep in mind that the person who wrote this verse is Solomon, who had seven hundred wives and three hundred concubines (official mistresses) on the side! This man who had engaged in sex with at least a thousand women had come to the realization that it's better to have only one wife. Solomon had learned the difference between love and lust. He had learned that satisfying his lust never really satisfied him. He knew that to be truly in love with one woman who was committed to him and him alone would have been far more fulfilling than to have many, many women who were simply willing to have sex with him. He wanted his son to experience love as it was intended to be experienced—not lust, which is a poor substitute for the real thing.

The Right Woman Is Worth the Wait

Still, some brothers will reason, "I need one woman who will party with me, one woman who will make a home for me, one woman who will enjoy sex as much as I do, one woman who will really listen to me, one woman who will go to games with me . . . ." And so, they develop relationships along the way with several women. What they don't realize is that if they find the *right* woman, they will have one person who meets all of those needs. This is the only way to be truly fulfilled because this is the way God designed it to be. When God decided to make a partner for Adam, He took only one rib from him because He made only one wife for him. God knew that one wife is all that any man needs.

Some men think they know better than God, so they have given up their ribs right and left. They have a rib down the street, a rib in their workplace, a rib at the club, a rib at school, a rib in another city, etc. They've got so many ribs that they don't remember where all of them are. What they don't understand is that the ribs protect the heart. If they have let go of a bunch of ribs in order to have a lot of women, they have left their hearts vulnerable. They are far more likely to end up with a broken heart, along with a messed-up life, because they thought they could improve on God's design.

By telling his son to drink from one well, Solomon is advising him to have only one wife. The water is an analogy. He is saying that he can be satisfied by that one well. He is telling his son that he needs a woman who can quench his thirst, fulfill his desires, and satisfy his needs—the same way that water satisfies a man who has been walking in the heat and desolation of a barren desert. Did you notice that Solomon changes the illustration from honey and oil to water? That's because he was saying that his son needs a woman who could meet his basic needs. That doesn't mean he can't also have the honey and the oil, but he needs to get it from the same place he gets his water. Some women can offer up the honey and oil on occasion when they feel like it, but they have no water to give. A man can live without honey and oil, but he can't live long without water.

Think about it. Let's say a man thinks he can live on honey alone, so he goes to a woman who will give him honey for an hour. But what then? Where does he go for heart-to-heart conversation? Where does he go for emotional support? Where does he go to think through the issues in his life? He will soon find that he needs a woman who can offer more than honey. Honey is sweet, but it is no substitute for water. Water refreshes, renews, and keeps us alive. Without it the organs in our body quit functioning and we die. A man needs to find a woman who can give him water as well as honey.

The *right* woman will be able to offer both. When speaking of the wife in verse 19, Solomon writes, "May her breasts satisfy you always, may you ever be intoxicated with her love." You need a wife who satisfies you sexually. A woman who withholds sex as punishment because her husband hasn't done what she wants is leaving a door open for him to be tempted outside the home. If a man eats all he wants in his own home, even if he passes by one restaurant after another, he won't stop because he has been satisfied at home. You need a woman who will meet your sexual needs.

Sex Was God's Idea

God gave you a strong sex drive, son. It is not something that is carnal or sinful. It is a gift from God. Listening to some church folk, you might think there is something wrong with you because you have a strong sex drive. That isn't true. You have a strong sex drive because God designed you like that. The very first commandment God gave man in the Bible is to have sex! Genesis 1:27 says, "So God created mankind in his own image, in the image of God he created them; male and female he created them." And the very next verse says, "God blessed them and said to them, 'Be fruitful and increase in number.'" Humankind's mission was to be fruitful and increase in number and the only way they could do that was by having sex. So God gave man a strong sex drive in order to do what God had commanded him to do.

Some Christians aren't even honest when talking to new converts. They tell them, "Now that you're a Christian, you are a new person, so you won't feel like you used to feel when you were out in the world. You won't have those same desires that you used to have." That's not true. Christ saves us from our sins, not from our sex drive, which is a gift from God. In fact, I believe that sexuality and spirituality are so closely connected that the more spiritual we become, the more sexual we will be.

This doesn't mean, however, that just because we're Christians, we engage in sex without being in a committed marriage relationship. But it means that because we are Christians, we are freed from old hang-ups, from false teaching that says sex is sinful, and from inhibitions that come from our misunderstanding about sex. Sex is a precious gift from God. Your sex drive is a gift to you from God so that you will be drawn into the kind of relationship that God desires for you with a loving wife.

Sex Is in Our DNA

You may be thinking, *But you don't understand how really strong my sex drive is. You don't realize how much time I spend thinking about sex every day.* Various studies have estimated the number of times a man thinks of sex throughout each day is anywhere from every five seconds, to ten minutes, to once or twice an hour. Of course, that number is influenced by whether or not the man is bored, whether or not he is in the presence of attractive women, etc. Regardless, the fact is that sex is often, very often, on the mind of every virile man. Son, you are not the only man who thinks about sex. Every man thinks about sex. It's part of our makeup. It's part of being a man. Some women don't understand that because most of them think of sex less often than men do. But son, if you are thinking of sex often throughout the day, you aren't abnormal—you're simply a man.

Remember that your sex drive is a gift. In itself, sex is good. It is God ordained. The only time sex is no longer good is when it's used outside of God's set parameters. The boundary that God set is that of marriage. God doesn't want us burning with passion. In fact, even to unmarried women and widows, 1 Corinthians 7:9 says, "But if they cannot control themselves, they should marry, for it is better to marry than to burn with passion." God doesn't want us burning with passion that cannot be directed into a loving sexual relationship with a spouse.

I really like the King James Version's rendering of Hebrews 13:4: "Marriage is honourable in all, and the bed undefiled." This says that sex in marriage is undefiled—that is, beautiful, good, and holy. Of course, that verse goes on to say, ". . .but whoremongers and adulterers God will judge." That means that what is so pure within marriage becomes the opposite outside of marriage. It becomes wrong, tainted, and worthy of God's judgment. Any sex outside of marriage is polluted. No matter how good it feels or how right in seems, it is wrong.

But within the marriage relationship, anything you and your wife agree to on a sexual basis is pure. There isn't only one position approved by God, while all others are outside His will. That would be like going into a cafeteria, being offered a whole array of appealing and delicious items, and coming out time and time again with a bowl of plain jello. Why would any couple do that—unless they truly both prefer jello? But you don't need to limit yourselves in order to somehow seem more spiritual. God is saying to you, "Go. Enjoy. I give this to you."

Three Great Reasons for Sex

Son, the three purposes of sex are procreation, recreation, and expression. Procreation simply means to be fruitful and multiply, or have children. Recreation and release is a second purpose of sex. When you read the Song of Solomon in the Bible, you will find a couple who enjoy having sex together, and it has nothing to do with procreation. Children are not mentioned as a reason for their having sex. They simply are attracted to each other's bodies and enjoy the feelings that come from the sexual activity. And they did not limit themselves to the bedroom, either. They also had sex in the living room, outside under a tree, in the dining area, in the garden, in the clefts of the rocks, in the vineyard, and elsewhere.

Now, hear me clearly. I would never suggest that anyone have sex outdoors because, at least in our state, it is illegal. It may be sanctioned by God and not immoral in His eyes, but society would take a very dim view of it. The point isn't about where you have sex, but that you learn to be playful with the activity. Learn to have fun with your spouse.

The third purpose of sex is expression. Remember that when God brought Eve to Adam, He said, "That is why a man leaves his father and mother and is united to his wife, and they become one flesh" (Genesis 2:24). The act of two becoming one is exactly what happens during sexual intercourse. The man enters the woman, and the two become one. It is an expression of their love. And they can express that love in any position, in any way, and at any time they both agree upon.

Patient and Passionate

You can never force any action upon your wife and say that it is love. You both have to agree. You may want to do something that fulfills a fantasy that you have, but if it makes her feel like a whore, or feel uncomfortable in any way, you need to let that idea go and focus on doing those things that say "love" to both of you.

Her feelings may stem from what her parents have taught her or from what she has learned in the church that she attended as a girl. Statistics say that one of every three women has been sexually assaulted sometime during their lifetime. Was your wife ever sexually assaulted? Is this something she wants to tell you, but isn't able to yet because she's still learning to trust you? Wherever her ideas have come from, you should never run roughshod over her feelings and insist upon doing something that lessens her self-esteem. That can never draw you closer or be considered an expression of love in her eyes. You must remember that 1 Corinthians 13:4 says, "Love is patient, love is kind."

Just because your wife isn't willing to do something now doesn't mean that she will never be willing to do it. You can read books together about sex from a Christian perspective. This can help open doors of communication and allow you both to learn to explore each other's bodies with a greater sense of freedom and joy. If there are serious issues that you can't work through, you can consult a doctor or Christian counselor to help you. The secret is that you have to grow as a couple.

But son, let me tell you something. Being a Christian doesn't mean that you can't have a good time with your wife in bed. You don't have to be boring just because you are Christian. That's why Solomon likens the wife to a baby deer in verse 19. She doesn't have to lie there quiet, immobile, half asleep, just letting sex happen to her. A baby deer is frisky. A baby deer romps and plays with abandon.

Your wife needs to be able to continually satisfy you with her breasts, but that doesn't mean that, once you are married, you can have sex on demand. There are many issues that affect one's sexual desire, such as sickness, stress, overwork, worry, PMS, or menopause. Couples go through different seasons when they may engage in sex more or less often for a period of time. But your wife needs to let you know that she desires you. She needs to want to express her love to you in the bedroom. She needs to offer you so much assurance of her love and her desire for you that, even if you are not having sex on a particular night, you still feel a sense of satisfaction. This woman pleases you. This woman turns you on. This woman gives herself totally to you. This woman is yours and you are hers.

Breasts Alone Are Not Enough

Keep in mind, too, son that breasts alone are not enough. You need to find a woman who can empathize with you, hold your hand and sit quietly with you, and show a willingness to listen without offering advice or judgment. You can't build a strong and healthy relationship just on breasts. Breasts alone are not enough. Breasts change. If your marriage is built solely on her breasts and the breasts change, you haven't got anything left. You need a woman who will captivate you with her love.

Not only do breasts change, son, but, believe it or not, there will come a season in your life when breasts won't be all that important to you. Hopefully, it won't be a long period of your life, but you can count on the fact that you will someday go through a time when breasts will not satisfy. It could be a physical issue; it might be an emotional situation; or it could be any area that preoccupies your mind and seems overwhelming.

I went through a season like that. When I was diagnosed with cancer, I was sent from one hospital to another and had one test after another. I was poked and prodded, had needles and tubes stuck in me, and was put in one machine after another. For the two months that all of this was going on, breasts were not important to me. But I thank God that I have a wife who would still captivate me, overwhelm me, and ravish me with her love.

It's crucial that you genuinely love the woman you marry, but it is just as important that you find a woman who will love you back. If you are the one doing all of the loving, that is a nonreciprocal relationship. It is dysfunctional. It will not work and will not satisfy either of you.

Look for Love

You need a woman who will evaluate your need and meet that need in a spirit of sacrificial love, even when she doesn't feel like doing it. She must understand your need for respect, your need for peace and quiet, your need for a gentle voice and words of kindness. She needs to know you intimately and love you just the way you are. Do not get trapped into marrying a woman who thinks that you will change once she puts a ring on your finger. You are just going to be more of what you already are, so you need to find a woman who will love you unconditionally. In 1 Corinthians 13:4-8 we read,

> Love is patient, love is kind. It does not envy, it does not boast, it is not proud. It does not dishonor others, it is not self-seeking, it is not easily angered, it keeps no record of wrongs. Love does not delight

in evil but rejoices with the truth. It always protects, always trusts, always hopes, always perseveres. Love never fails.

You need a woman who will be patient with you and kind to you. You want a woman who isn't boastful or proud. She doesn't put others down and try to promote herself. She doesn't get angry easily and doesn't keep track of all your mistakes and failures. She is protective, trusting, hopeful, and enduring. You can always count on her love to be there for you. Just when you need her love the most, it never fails. My wife Sharon and I are still married after twenty-six years because she is a woman who doesn't keep count of things I do wrong. Had she kept track of them, we would have gotten a divorce a long time ago. First Peter 4:8 says, "Love covers over a multitude of sins." You need a woman who will love you just as you are.

Passion under Control

I followed a story about Carolina Panthers' Steve Smith, one of the top wide receivers in the NFL. He plays with so much intensity, which is why he's so good. But sometimes that passion gets out of control. For instance, one time when he scored a touchdown, a player pushed him as he went over the goal line and Smith began fighting. Both benches emptied and got involved in the fray because Smith let his passion get out of control. Another time at a team meeting, he got in trouble for jumping on one of his teammates and received a two-game suspension. These are examples of passion out of control.

But there are times, however, when Steve Smith's passion is under control and directed in positive ways. He has an affinity towards the poor. He grew up in poverty and, as a child, went through a period when he was homeless, so now he helps the poor and the homeless. Modeling Jesus' servanthood, he and others washed the feet of four hundred homeless people and provided them with new shoes. That is passion under control.

Come As You Are

Reporters once interviewed Steve Smith's wife and asked her, "Does your husband have the same intensity at home that he has on the field?" She responded, "Well, I can't say that, although my husband is a very intense man. But my husband knows when he comes home that he can just be himself." Son, that's the kind of wife you need—one who accepts you as you are and will let you be yourself at home.

For too many men, it's like Halloween every night. (I hate Halloween anyhow. I don't think we need to be celebrating demons, devils, and ghouls. We're Christians.) But some men experience Halloween every night in their own homes. On their way home, these men are thinking, *What costume am I going to wear tonight? What mask am I going to have to wear?* When it gets to this point, a husband and wife never really express who they truly are, only who they're pretending to be. At some point, a man is going to get tired of Halloween and take that mask off, and his wife won't know how to deal with that. You want to marry your best friend—somebody you can love who will love you back. You want someone who can satisfy you, sympathize with you, and allow you to be who you are when you come home.

But you can't have that kind of love until you have the love of God in your heart. It starts with a personal relationship with God. You cannot love yourself or anyone else right until you have things right with God. God loves you so much. He loves you just the way you are. Jesus died on the cross to forgive you of every sin and draw you into a relationship with God. Son, develop that relationship with God. Then, and only then, can you know love with a woman the way that God intended.

An Example to Consider: Elkanah

Please take out your Bible and read 1 Samuel 1.

Son, being the right man is just as important as finding the right woman. In 1 Samuel 1, we read the story of how God blessed Hannah, who was barren, with a son. Often when that story is told, the role of Elkanah, her husband, is overlooked. In the times and culture in which Elkanah and Hannah lived, a woman who could not have a baby was considered inferior, even worthless. Polygamy was acceptable then, so a husband could easily set her aside and favor another wife over her. Since children were a sign of God's blessing, a woman who could not bear children might cause people to wonder, *How has she sinned that God will not bless her?* Infertility brought great pain, depression and even desperate actions, as when Sarah offered her maidservant to Abraham to bear a child that she mistakenly thought could become like her own.

Elkanah's wife was in this barren position. She could not bear him a child. He had another wife who had given him children, and that wife ridiculed Hannah, making her feel even more miserable. So, what was Elkanah's response to her? Did he ridicule her too? Did he set her aside for the other wife? Did he ask her what sin she was hiding that caused God to keep her from having children? Did he secretly love her, but publicly denounce her to save face? No. He genuinely loved her, and his response was to try to reassure and comfort her. First Samuel 1:8 says, "Her husband Elkanah would say to her, 'Hannah, why are you weeping? Why don't you eat? Why are you downhearted? Don't I mean more to you than ten sons?'"

Elkanah was a man of God. Verse 3 says, "Year after year this man went up from his town to worship and sacrifice to the Lord Almighty." And he did not leave Hannah at home alone, as one disgraced. In fact, when distributing his portion of the peace offering, he gave Hannah a double portion as a sign of his love for her. In verse 19 we read, "Elkanah made love to his wife Hannah." But this time, "the Lord remembered" Hannah, and in nine months she gave birth to Samuel. While this son must have been very precious to Elkanah—the child of his beloved Hannah—when Hannah told him that she was going to take him to the temple to dedicate him to the Lord's service, Elkanah responded, "Do what seems best to you." He did not stand in the way of her offering their best to God. And 1 Samuel 2:21 says, "And the Lord was gracious to Hannah; she gave birth to three sons and two daughters." Because of Elkanah's faithfulness to God and to his wife, he could rejoice as God blessed Hannah and him with even more children.

Dear God,

Once I have *found* the right person, help me to *be* the right person. Help me to be faithful to You and to my wife. Teach me how to love her even as I want to be loved—unconditionally and with passion, patience, kindness, and self-sacrifice. Help me to work to make our home a place of peace and joy for us both. Amen.

CHAPTER 6

Making Sense of Life

My child, if you have put up security for a friend's debt

    or agreed to guarantee the debt of a stranger —

if you have trapped yourself by your agreement

    and are caught by what you said —

follow my advice and save yourself,

    for you have placed yourself at your friend's mercy.

Now swallow your pride;

    go and beg to have your name erased.

Don't put it off; do it now!

    Don't rest until you do.

Save yourself like a gazelle escaping from a hunter,

    like a bird fleeing from a net.

Take a lesson from the ants, you lazybones.

    Learn from their ways and become wise!

Proverbs 6:1-6 NLT

Written for Broken People

The word "crazy" that we use in English etymologically comes originally from a French word that means to shatter, to make flawed, to break. You've heard of a mental breakdown. Because, as Romans 3:23 tells us, "All have sinned and fall short of the glory of God," there are things that many of us have done in the past that have left us shattered, fractured, and broken. We have been left broken because of the guilt and consequences that came from bad decisions we made. Every choice has a consequence. When we make choices outside the will of God, the consequences leave us broken.

In Proverbs 1:8 Solomon writes, "Listen, my son, to your father's instruction." Solomon is speaking the words of Proverbs to his son or sons. Since Solomon was a king, he was also talking to young men who were going to be the future leaders of Israel. He was trying to teach them how to make sense out of life. And we know that the Bible was written for men and women in all times and all places, so we need to apply to our own lives the lessons that Solomon was teaching his son.

What's in a Name?

In chapter 6, Solomon is saying that some of us have already gotten ourselves into trouble. Some of us have signed up for things we couldn't handle. We signed a contract saying we would do certain things or pay back a certain amount of money for a purchase, but then we couldn't do it. Now, we are realizing there are consequences for our actions that affect our reputation. Our name is in jeopardy of not being respected. Proverbs 22:1 says, "A good name is more desirable than great riches; to be esteemed is better than silver or gold." Since a good name is better than gold, if I have not been faithful in maintaining my reputation, I have actually devalued my name.

A good name is so important. At some point, you are going to want to get married and give a woman your name. But if she is the intelligent and worthy woman that you desire, she is going to check your name out. She isn't someone with an inferiority complex who would be grateful that any man wants to marry her. No, the woman you choose is going to be a woman of substance who knows that she is bringing a lot into this relationship. So, she won't enter into it blindly. She's going to make sure that your name carries the same value as her own name.

Your Today Affects Your Tomorrow

Someday, you are also going to want to buy a house. The mortgage company is going to look at your name to see if they can trust you to repay the mortgage. Someday, you are going to want to buy a new car. The dealer is going to check out your name to make sure you will make those car payments. And, if your name doesn't qualify you for excellent credit, you are going to end up paying more for that car because you are a greater risk for the company.

Someday, you are going to want to be involved in ministry. Believe me, a church, parachurch ministry, or nonprofit organization is going to check out your name when you express interest in working for them. They are going to seek references and want a recommendation from your pastor and other church leaders so that they know that you are worthy of the ministry that they might entrust to you. They want to know that if your name is attached to theirs, it will further lift up their work, not tear it down.

In the financial realm, when we sign up for something we can't handle, it not only devalues our name, but it also affects our resources. When we borrow money, that amount is called the "principal." But when we pay the money back, we have to pay more than just the principal, more than the amount we borrowed. The additional amount we have to pay is called "interest." That is the amount charged for using someone else's money. When we borrow money, we become indebted to the lender. The last part of Proverbs 22:7 tells us that "the borrower is slave to the lender."

You may wonder how that plays out in the twenty-first century. When a collection is taken in your church, you know it is for the operation of the ministry, to help reach out to the needy in the community, and to engage in the Lord's work in many ways. You really want to give. You have a heart to support the ministry. But you can't give anything. Why? Because your masters, the lenders, won't let you. They determine where your money goes every month. You may want to help victims of a hurricane or tornado. You may want to help support a child in a third world country. You may want to reach out to assist someone in your own family or among your friends who is facing a crisis. But you can't do any of that. Why? Because your masters, the lenders, tell you that, regardless of anything else, you have to pay them a certain amount each month. Until you get out of debt, you are a slave to your lenders.

Financial Decisions Can Hurt

Being in debt also affects relationships. The number one reason for divorce in America today involves money. It isn't always a matter of not having it. Often, it's a matter of deciding what to do with it when you do have it. When one person wants to save and be responsible with the family income and the other wants to spend irresponsibly, it brings division in the home. When one person wants to cater to his or her own desires—for shoes, clothes, a pastime, entertainment, or whatever—at the expense of meeting the other person's needs or desires, that selfishness brings division. Our choices in life can bring guilt, and consequences that are very, very negative.

Indebtedness can also affect relationships with friends or extended family members. Remember, verses 1 and 2 of Proverbs 6 say, "My child, if you have put up security for a friend's debt or agreed to guarantee the debt of a stranger— if you have trapped yourself by your agreement and are caught by what you said . . ." He is speaking to someone who has agreed to co-sign a loan with someone else. If you have a friend for whom you have co-signed, that means the transaction would not have happened without your signature. You have enabled this person to do something that he or she could not have done on his or her own. You threw your weight behind the transaction enabling it to happen. It is your name that got the loan to go through or got the purchase on credit, and it is also your name that will be devalued if the payments are late or the person defaults. When people ask me to co-sign for them, I am thinking, *If the bank, which has billions of dollars won't trust you, I'm sorry, I can't help you. I've only got a few thousand. If the one with billions won't take the risk, I surely can't afford to do so either.*

Be Careful What You Sign

Now, some of us have not signed up for anything financial, but we have signed up for something relational that we couldn't handle. We signed up for something that we should never have signed up for, such as adultery or other kinds of sexual immorality. Or we may have entered into a relationship with someone that requires us to do something unethical, something that would compromise our Christian principles. Our names should never be used to enter into a relationship that is outside the will of God. No matter how hard we try to "handle" it, we never can because it was never part of God's will for our lives in the first place.

Son, make sure that you are careful before you put your name on anything. In fact, be careful about anything that you put in writing— whether it is an email, a blog, a tweet, a Facebook entry or whatever it is. You undoubtedly know someone who got in trouble because of something that he or she posted online. Perhaps it was a student who got in trouble at your school, a colleague at your workplace who was fired, or even a family member or friend who lost a significant relationship because of something they posted online that they didn't intend for others to read. Lives have been shattered and relationships broken because of something that was carelessly put in writing.

Change Is Possible

Son, know that if you have already experienced that brokenness or are already living a shattered life because of past mistakes, there is still hope. If you are already in trouble because of bad choices you have made, you don't have to despair. If you have already fallen and your dreams have been dashed, you don't have to stay down and defeated. God can bring you out of any circumstance. God can bring healing to your brokenness. God can give you a new vision for your life and all that He wants to accomplish through you.

Don't give up, son. Just take hold of God's outstretched hand and let Him help you. He didn't stay with you through this situation just to leave you in it. If that had been His intention, He would have walked away when you first messed up. But He didn't. He stayed so that He could help you out when you finally came to the realization that You need His help. He is here to help you even now in this moment.

An article in the newspaper recently made the point that the recession led to more graduations among young people ages twenty-five to twenty-nine. When the economy went bad, young people came to a wise understanding of the situation and said to themselves, *If I'm going to make it, I'm going to need some education.* So, they either decided to go to school for the first time or return to school to get their diplomas and degrees to make them more competitive in the job market. The reality prior to this massive return to school was that, for the first time ever, the next generation would have less education than the prior generation.

What I find great about the action taken by our young people is that they learned from the bad situation they were facing. They saw what was happening to others because of the recession and decided they didn't want to end up going through life working minimum wage jobs and struggling financially. So they did something about it. It's tragic when people don't learn from what is going on around them.

Proverbs 6:6 (NLT) says, "Take a lesson from the ants, you lazybones. Learn from their ways and become wise!" I've already talked with you about the importance of formal education. But it is also necessary for you to learn lessons from life. This is true no matter how old you are or how well educated you are. There is always more to learn. Learn from what is going on around you. Watch what happens to others. Watch what others do. Look at what leads to love, peace and joy, and what leads to bitterness, anger, and defeat. Then—and this is the most important part—*do* what leads to the positive results you want to see in your life.

Get Over It!

In thinking about making sense of life, Proverbs 6:5 (NLT) urges us to at least have as much sense as a gazelle. It says, "Save yourself like a gazelle escaping from a hunter, like a bird fleeing from a net." Gazelles have the ability to jump thirty feet into the air. They recognize that situations arise in which they can only get the victory if they *get over it*. What they do in the physical realm, I would urge us to do in the spiritual and emotional realms as well.

We need to follow this advice anytime someone has brought pain, suffering, and sorrow into *our* lives. If somebody dogged you, get over it. If somebody lied about you, get over it. If somebody spread rumors about you, get over it. If somebody manipulated you, get over it. If somebody said, "I do," and then didn't, get over it. If you were fired unjustly, that's terrible, but get over it. That person should never have walked out of your life, but get over it.

That person should never have left you to raise your children alone, but get over it. Life is full of unfairness. If we let it keep us down, we will go throughout our lives bitter, depressed, and defeated. We must have the same sense that a gazelle has when knowing danger is present. Get over it!

This advice is true not only for times in which others mess up and hurt us, but it's especially true for us in areas in which we have messed up. Maybe we have entered into a contract, or a relationship, or a situation that we weren't able to handle and we have ended up broken, miserable, and overwhelmed. If that is the case, we can't afford to stay in that place of danger and defeat a minute longer. We have to rise up and get over it!

Think Like a Gazelle

Let's look more closely at what happens when *we* are the ones who fail. If you made a promise but didn't keep it, if you made a commitment but didn't follow through, if you said you would do one thing but then did something else, you likely know the misery of guilt and shame. Only someone totally given over to evil does not have a conscience that becomes uneasy in the midst of moral/ethical failure. Be thankful when your conscience is active and you feel guilty after you've done something wrong. That means that God hasn't given up on you. God is trying to pull you back into fellowship with Him and into right relationship with others.

You may find, as I have, that it is easier to get over someone doing something against you than it is for you to get over it when you have done something that has hurt or offended someone else. I have grown in my walk with God so I know how to forgive other people. Despite how someone may have offended me, I know how not to let it change the way I relate to that person. I have learned that I don't have to be mean, vindictive, and cold to someone who has hurt or offended me. I know how to genuinely forgive and get over it.

But the hard part for me is getting over it when I'm the one who messed up. When the guilt is on *me*, I have a hard time thinking like a gazelle. Yet, I have come a long way in that area because I know this one thing: God will forgive me and give me another chance. Son, everybody who has ever served God, except for Jesus, has messed up in some way. But the Lord forgave each one of them and gave them another chance. Abraham lied. Moses murdered somebody. David committed adultery, killed somebody, and had a baby out of wedlock. Peter denied Jesus three times.

Son, I have failed at times in my life too. Even though I have a desire to serve God fully and I love God with all my heart, there have been times when I have let God down. And I felt miserable. Like the prodigal son in the parable Jesus told, I felt unworthy to be called a son of my heavenly Father. I was ashamed that, as one called to serve in ministry, I had failed God. But God forgave me and gave me another chance. By His grace, I was able to get over it.

You can too, son. This is not true because you promise to be good. It's not true because you do a lot of good deeds to offset the wrong you have done. It's true because of what Jesus did for us— *only* because of what Jesus did for us. He took our sins to a cross on Calvary. Because He died, we can live. Because of what He did, we can find grace, mercy, and forgiveness. Because Jesus died and rose again, we can put our past behind us and start fresh again. Like a gazelle, we *can* get over it.

Run Like a Gazelle, Too

Another ability that the gazelle has, in addition to jumping, is running. A gazelle can run up to sixty miles per hour. So, when it finds itself in a precarious situation, it has enough sense just to run. Son, learn from your past mistakes and follow the example of the gazelle. When you see something coming that you know you can't handle—run!

When you are at a store getting ready to pay cash for your purchase, and the clerk begins to press you to sign up for a credit card—run! When you are at a ballgame and someone is walking through the lobby offering a free t-shirt with your team's logo if you sign up for a credit card—run! When you're at the airport and someone tells you that you will get bonus miles if you sign up for a credit card—run!

When you see a beautiful woman who is sexy, sweet and smooth, but she is trying to seduce you, trying to make you forget that you're a man of God, trying to satisfy her own need for attention by leading you astray—run! Don't sit around talking with her, flirting with her, exchanging numbers with her, making plans to meet, connecting on Facebook, emailing, or tweeting—RUN!

That's what the apostle Paul told us to do. First Corinthians 6:18 says, "Flee from sexual immorality." Run from it! That's one of those situations you can't reason your way through. You can't talk your way through. You can't even pray your way through it in that moment. If you are praying silently, *God, help me not to yield to this temptation,* all the while you are looking lustfully at this woman's body, your so-called "prayers" are in vain. If you are saying in your mind, *God, help me; God, help me; God help me,* all the while standing there as she is enticing you with her eyes, tempting you with her lips, and moving her body close to yours, you aren't really praying. You are a double-minded man. James 1:7 says, "That person should not expect to receive anything from the Lord." You aren't praying. You're like a drowning man who yells "Help!" as he's going under but makes no attempt to move his arms or kick his feet. In a situation in which the temptation is right in front of you, all you can do to get away is to run.

Don't Go It Alone

Now, gazelles are social animals. They run in herds, not alone. They know they can't make it by themselves. You don't see gazelles wandering alone. They know they need others to make it in this life. They know there is safety in numbers. Yet there are some human beings who believe they are smarter than gazelles, but they don't get it. They think *they* don't need anybody. They think they can make it through life all by themselves. That is a trick of the enemy. Our spiritual enemy knows that if we go off by ourselves, we become easy targets.

When we are by ourselves, our minds become vulnerable to attack because we don't have anyone else to help us think clearly or to challenge our thinking when it is heading away from thinking the thoughts of Christ. When we are by ourselves, our spirit becomes vulnerable to attack, and without others to cheer us along the way, we easily become discouraged and depressed.

When we are by ourselves, our bodies also become vulnerable to attack. We can easily be tempted in ways that cause us to respond according to our animalistic lusts and cravings for things that are unhealthy for us. When we are by ourselves, we become totally self*ish*—thinking only about what *we* want, what satisfies *our* desires, and what will make *us* happy. We need each other to be our best selves.

Son, life is too big to handle by yourself. When Jesus prayed in John 17:11, He prayed, "Holy Father, protect them by the power of your name, the name you gave me, so that they may be one as we are one." He didn't want us wandering around unprotected. And God certainly does not want His ministry carried on in this world by a bunch of Lone Rangers.

In Ephesians 4:11-12, Paul writes of the various types of ministers needed to prepare God's people to serve: apostles, prophets, evangelists, pastors, and teachers. But then he says, in verse 13, "Until we all reach unity in the faith." God expects us to work together, not alone. And as we do so, Paul reminds us in verses 3 through 6 in that same chapter, "Make every effort to keep the unity of the Spirit through the bond of peace. There is one body and one Spirit, just as you were called to one hope when you were called; one Lord, one faith, one baptism; one God and Father of all, who is over all and through all and in all." There is only one God, and we are all a part of that one God, that one Body.

Members of the Same Body

In Romans 12:4-5, the apostle Paul clarifies that principle: "For just as each of us has one body with many members, and these members do not all have the same function, so in Christ we, though many, form one body, and each member belongs to all the others." Each member belongs to all the others.

We must understand the importance of being connected. We never see a leg walking down the street on its own. No, that leg needs to be connected to the rest of the body if it is going to survive and function as it is intended to function. We should thank God for the church, because we don't have to be out there all by ourselves— fractured, broken and flawed. Instead, we are connected to every other Christian all over the world, and most intimately with those in our local church, where you worship and serve on a regular basis.

Michael Jones, pastor of Progressive Missionary Baptist Church in Indianapolis, tells one of my favorite illustrations. He saw this intriguing segment about stallions and jackasses on an Animal Planet television program. The story pointed out that whenever a coyote, a natural enemy of a jackass, approaches a bunch of jack-asses, their owner has to run out to protect them because they can't protect themselves against this predator. The reason is that they don't work together well. They get part of it right: they come together for protection. But the problem is that they put their hind ends together. So, when they start kicking to protect themselves, they are kicking each other, not the coyote.

Smart as a Stallion

When a herd of stallions is in that same situation, however, the owner doesn't have to be there to protect them. They can protect themselves. The difference is that they put their *heads* together. So, when a coyote comes to attack one of them, they are all kicking up a storm and they either hit the coyote or scare it away. They are kicking the enemy, not each other. We can learn a lesson from them. When life gets hard and the enemy comes to attack one of us in the church, we've got to put our heads together and work together to attack the enemy, not each other.

We can see this happening in the political realm. President Barack Obama was elected to another term in office because African Americans, Latinos, singles, gays, young people, and the poor determined that they were not going to get into a frenzy kicking each other. Instead, they decided that they were going to put their heads together and work together to get a victory. We need to see this happen in the church—to get a victory for Jesus.

Bird Sense

Now, I have written about having the sense of a gazelle and the sense of a stallion, but I would urge you also to have the sense of a bird. A lot of things can put birds in jeopardy. But birds know to rise above any snare that could entrap and destroy them. Son, there are a lot of things in this world that can ensnare and destroy you as well. You need to avoid the snares, whether they are political, social, economic, judicial, educational, etc. These are systemic traps.

It isn't fair that racial and economic biases exist within the judicial system. It isn't right that, on average, if your skin and your

225

wallet meet a certain criteria, you are treated one way; but if not, there is another set of rules that is applied. Now, you already know how it works. You know that if you get involved in that system, you will face injustices. So, the way to avoid being ensnared is to stay out of the system. Rise above it. Don't get caught in it. The only way a bird is ensnared is not because someone raises a net into the sky to catch it. No, a bird is entrapped when it flies so low that a net can reach it.

There are traps that are a part of all social systems. If one is wealthy and part of the majority culture, the system favors that person. It is easier for those who meet the hidden criteria for success in any of our systems. But that doesn't mean you cannot break through the system. Look all around you and you will see people who have overcome. Read your history books and you will meet people who overcame what appeared to be insurmountable obstacles. How did they do that? They learned from the birds. They learned how to fly above the traps and snares that were there to hold them back and make them fail.

A New System

Remember, son, you are not alone. Jesus has a system that helps us to rise above the systems of this world. What does that look like? Paraphrasing from Jesus' illustration in Matthew 25, "I was hungry, and you developed a feeding program to make sure I had something to eat. I was hungry, and you provided free breakfasts and free lunches so that I could think when I was attending school to get my lessons. I was hungry, and you provided job opportunities so that I could go to work and earn money to feed my family myself. I was homeless, but you provided adequate housing so that I was sheltered from the elements outside. I was in prison, but after I paid my debt to society, you came up with a program that allowed me to reenter the community with the support I needed to enable me to become a productive citizen. I was sick, but even though I had a pre-existing condition, you provided healthcare for me so that I could get well."

God has a different system from this world's system. His system says, "Love your enemies, do good to those who hate you, bless those who curse you, pray for those who mistreat you" (Luke 6:27-28). You have to rise above the traps of the world. You have to live according to God's system because the world's system will pass away, but God's system endures forever.

Someone's Out to Get You

Not only are there systemic traps, but there are also satanic traps set for you. Ephesians 6:12 points out, "For our struggle is not against flesh and blood, but against the rulers, against the authorities, against the powers of this dark world and against the spiritual forces of evil in the heavenly realms." It is important for you to recognize how the enemy sets traps. One thing that happens often is that the enemy ensnares you when you are young, but you don't realize the consequences until you are older.

The enemy delights in entrapping a young person because he knows that if he waits until that person is older, wiser, more mature, more experienced older version of the young man won't be so vulnerable. He won't listen to the lies of the enemy so readily. He will better discern the voice of the enemy from the voice of God, so he won't be tricked so easily. His values will have deepened and his priorities will have changed, so he won't be so open to what the enemy has to offer. But if Satan gets the person while he is young, he can often continue to wreak havoc throughout that man's lifetime.

Why did the enemy try to destroy Moses when Moses was just a baby? Because he knew it would be easier to destroy Moses as a baby than when he was an adult, called of God, standing before Pharaoh, saying, "Let my people go." But if he can't destroy a young person, he will try to deceive him. If he can get a young person to do what he says at this point in his life, he won't have to worry about trying to defeat him later on when he is wiser and more mature.

Don't be naïve, son. Satan does not come to you with horns and a pitchfork, shouting, "Boo!" Second Corinthians 11:14 says, "Satan himself masquerades as an angel of light." That means that he looks attractive. He can masquerade in many forms, but he will always be trying to tempt you, even as he tempted Adam, to listen to what he said instead of what God said, to obey him rather than God.

Premarital Sex Robs Your Marriage

While you are a young person, Satan might say to you, "Listen, man, you are young and single. Go sow your wild oats while you can. You'll be married someday and stuck with just one woman. Don't waste any time now. This is your one and only chance to be free. Besides, God won't care. He knows it's a different day from when the Bible was written. He understands your heart. Go out and enjoy yourself while you can." So you hook up with one woman after another, having sex with everyone you can. In fact, you pride yourself on being able to sweettalk women into the bedroom. And, all the while, Satan is whispering in your ear: "Nice going. You're a real man. It's okay. You're single."

But when you mature and really do become a man, you begin to realize that this life you've been living is empty and void. You recognize the difference now between the lust that you are experiencing and the love that you really want to have. You are tired of shallow, easy women and you long for a relationship with a woman of substance, someone to love, to protect, to be the mother of your children. Eventually, you find the woman with whom you want to spend the rest of your life.

You wait until you are married and then you come together to express your love to her through sex. But the problem is that you've never used sex as a means of expressing love. You've only used it to satisfy your lust. You suddenly realize that you don't know

229

how to express love through sex. You can't make the transition. The enemy has been deceiving you for years. You became really good at going through the motions, but now that you are married and you want your sexual relationship to have meaning and to be special, you don't know how.

Likewise, there are married women who had multiple relationships while they were single. They let men do all sorts of things with them during sex because they were living only according to their lusts. They felt they had a right to do that because they were single and free. But when a woman who has lived like that marries, she also finds that she doesn't know how to express love through sex. She can go through the motions, as she's always done, but she doesn't know how to make a deeper, inner connection with her husband. Her mind has been confused by the years of letting men use her simply to satisfy their own lusts. She doesn't know what a *loving* sexual relationship looks like. The enemy tricked her into making choices when she was young that she is paying for now that she has come to a new level of maturity.

Our Past Catches Up with Us

The enemy comes at us when we are unemployed. If we aren't careful, we may use that as an excuse for making bad decisions and doing foolish things, but we don't realize the full consequences until later on. We may do something illegal and feel pretty cocky because all we got was probation, just a slap on the wrist. We think we beat the system. But then down the road, we find a job we really want. We know we've got a good chance of getting it, but then the employer does a background check. The consequences of our past decisions suddenly overtake us as we are passed over for someone without a record.

You have to understand this, son. The enemy tempts you to do foolish things in the *now* in order to mess up your life in your *not yet*. He knows the consequences later on will be far greater than any immediate consequence for your actions. So, he tempts you in the *now* to do something opposed to the will of God. But you don't feel the consequences until you are in your *not yet*—in your future. And you are tempted so easily because you think your *now* is all that there ever will be. You don't think ahead and realize how your current decisions can affect you down the road.

You don't stop to think that Jesus has a better future for you than you can even imagine—*if* you let Him direct you in the now. All you know is that you are broke in the now. You are uneducated in the now. In the now, you are unemployed; you have no power in this world. You feel like a failure in the now. But, son, your *now* isn't going to be your *always*. You see, in your *not yet*, God has something for you.

In the not yet, you're not broke, you're rich. You're not sick, you're healthy. You're not unemployed, you own your own company. In the not yet, you're not by yourself, you have a wife and children. You aren't impotent, you're influential. Son, the enemy knows that God has not abandoned you. The enemy knows that he has to take you out now because, if he doesn't, God's going to turn your life around so that you won't be tempted by the things that tempt you now. If the enemy waits, you will begin to see God at work in your life and you won't be interested in what the enemy has to offer.

Be On Guard When You're Tired

Remember, you must have bird sense — sense enough to fly high, live high, and rest high out of reach of the enemy. Birds build their nests on mountaintops, in treetops, and other high places where they are safe. In the same way, you need to build your home on higher ground, not living a lowdown life where you are easy prey for the enemy. Even when you rest, you have to stay in a safe place, above your enemy. Sometime you get so tired because you are working hard, taking care of your responsibilities, and keeping God first in your life. Sometimes, you get so tired that you feel like saying, "I've had enough." It's sometimes when we rest that we become the most vulnerable. When we rest, we let down our guard.

When we're tired, we are tempted to choose things that we wouldn't even consider otherwise. We may think that we have earned one day just to go wild. When we're tired, we may think that just a little marijuana would soothe our spirits and help us to feel better. We may be tempted to drink to the point that we will have no worries. We may be tempted to watch "just a little" porn to release some tension. All the while, we are deceiving ourselves by thinking, *God knows my heart. God knows I love Him. God understands the pressure I've been under and the stress I've been feeling. God knows I've earned this break from my routine.* Those thoughts are from the enemy, who knows that any lowdown living on our part will make us easy prey.

Follow the Son

I did a little study about bird migration. Birds have an inner sense that lets them know it is time to move south. They know when the weather is changing and that it's going to be too cold for them to stay in that area. So they take off and fly to a warmer climate. But how do they know where to go? How do they know to fly in one direction and not another? How do they know what their destination is? Birds don't have GPS systems attached to their wings. They don't have maps. They can't Google for directions. They can't stop at a service station to find out that they have to turn right after three blocks and then go left to I65 and take it south. No, they don't have access to all that information, so how do they know? I learned that their migration patterns have to do with the magnetic field on earth. The birds sense the magnetic field, and they follow it from the north to the south.

To further understand how the birds function, scientists conducted a research project in which they manipulated the magnetic field. As a result, the birds in Canada that were supposed to fly to South America were flying instead in the opposite direction. But after flying two thousand miles in the wrong direction, they suddenly made a U-turn and started flying back in the right direction, so they made it to their destination. But how did they know they were going in the wrong direction? How did they know to turn around? That's because the birds also use the sun as a compass. When these birds saw that the sun wasn't where it was supposed to be, they knew it wasn't the sun that was in the wrong place, because the sun doesn't move. They knew *they* were the ones in the wrong place, so they had the sense to turn around.

Similarly, the Enemy has manipulated the spiritual field on the earth in an attempt to get you to think that right is wrong and wrong is right. He wants you to think that up is down and down is up. He tries to make you think that you can be successful without working. He wants you to think that you can get rich without laboring. He wants you to believe that it is okay to have sex before you marry, to have children before you get married, and to live with a woman without being married. He has manipulated the spiritual field to deceive you.

Have the sense of birds, son. Don't keep going the wrong direction. Turn around. Look to the Son for your guidance. The Son of God is never in the wrong place. If anyone is out of order, it's you.

But you don't have to keep heading the wrong way. Do a U-turn and follow the Son.

A Lesson from the Ants

Another living creation that has a lesson for you is the ant. You also need to have the sense of an ant. Ants work hard. They aren't lazy. You see, ants know they can't jump high or run fast like a gazelle. They know they can't fly high in the sky or build nests in treetops like birds. But they don't focus on what they *can't* do, but on what they *can* do. Ants know they can work their way through anything. They create intricate and extensive underground chambers through their patience and strength. In fact, ants depend on their strength for their survival. They can lift twenty times their own weight.

Son, you can lift anything that you need to lift when you use the strength God has given you. And you can work your way through anything as you draw on the power of God in your life. When you accepted Jesus as your Savior, the Holy Spirit moved into your life. The Spirit equips you, enables you, empowers you, and energizes you. You can say, as Paul did in Philippians 4:13, "I can do all this through him who gives me strength."

Notice, too, that ants don't try to make it through life alone. They live and work in colonies. They specialize in their work. There are worker aunts, soldier aunts, leaf-cutting ants, fruit-cutting ants, and others. They all have something that each of them can do. They use their specialty to develop unity within the colony so that they can have some efficiency. They don't get jealous or envious when they see another ant doing things they can't do. Instead, they realize that they can do more together than they could alone, so they each do what they can do and the entire colony benefits. It is their diversity that produces their unity. We need to learn from the ants. We've got to stop fighting against each other and learn to stand with one another.

Make It Do What It Do

We've also got to be sure that we are doing the thing that God has called and equipped us to do. What is your specialty? What is it that you can do to help the body of Christ? Don't tell me, "Nothin'." God has given at least one spiritual gift to each Christian. No one Christian has every gift, but every Christian has at least one gift. You've got to discover, develop, and demonstrate that gift. And that takes time. Author Malcolm Gladwell says that it takes ten thousand hours to become an expert at anything. You can't sit on the sidelines and think that somehow you're going to master something. You'd better get started.

Ray is one of my favorite movies. Jamie Foxx portrays Ray Charles so well in that movie that I forgot it wasn't really Ray Charles on the screen. He looked like him, had his same voice, used his same mannerisms, sang like him, and played like him. At one point in the movie, Ray Charles was in the studio, and his backup singers got mad at him. They said they were quitting and they all ran out the door. They must have forgotten that Ray was operating in his specialty. He was operating in the gift God had given him. Others in the studio asked him, "Ray, what are you going to do now? All of your backup singers have left you."

He responded, "I'm getting ready to produce my song."

"But how are you going to do that? Who's going to sing the backup?"

"I'm going to sing the backup *and* the lead."

"So, you're going to sing alto and soprano?"

"Yeah, I'm going to sing it all."

"But how are you going to do it?"

"I'm going to make it do what it do, baby. I'm going to make it do what it do."

When folk laugh at your specialty, you don't have to get upset about that. Just tell them, "I'm going to make it do what it do, baby." You've got to get some ant sense.

Be Money Smart

Ants also save up their resources. They do a lot of hard work and gather food in the summer, but they don't consume everything that they gather. They save some for the winter. They know the winter is coming. They know they must have some food set aside to hold them during the winter months.

We have experienced a lot of economic downturns in our country. Some of the people in the church I pastor lost their jobs. Not just one, but several people came up to me at various times and told me they had been out of work for four months, six months, or longer. I usually respond initially by letting them know how sorry I am for what they are going through, and offering to pray for them. But some of them have stopped me, saying, "Oh no, Pastor, I'm not coming to ask you for help. I'm coming to testify."

"What do you mean *testify?*"

"Well, I've been out of work for six months and only recently got a new job. But I was able to make it during that period because I listened to you. You taught us to save at least six months' to a year's salary just in case something happened to keep us from working over a period of time. I followed your advice and saved that money, so even though I was out of work for six months, I was able to keep paying my bills and meeting my needs. Now I've just found a job that pays more than the job I had."

The reason these folks made it is because they didn't consume everything they got. They had ant sense. Son, if you save in the good times, you will be able to make it in the bad times.

Wisdom Is As Wisdom Does

There's one last thing I want to point out to you about ants: Ants are social beings. They don't go roaming by themselves. There are always other ants nearby. Ants will fight to the death for the queen and the colony. Some men could take a lesson from those ants, and show a willingness to fight for their queen and for their home and children. If the enemy attacks your marriage or home life, don't walk away or give in. You fight *for* your queen. You don't fight *with* your queen. Be willing to fight that enemy for your wife, your family, your home life, your church and your community.

The first five chapters of Proverbs offer wisdom principles you'll need when you reach chapter 6. Now, you have to *apply* what you've learned. You must have the wisdom to know what mode to go into—gazelle, bird, or ant mode. My iPad has a multiplicity of modes, including a sleep mode, restore mode, recovery mode, and music mode, but I still need the intelligence to know which mode I want to use.

Remember that no matter how much wrong you've done in the past, God can still forgive you. You don't have to stay messed up. You don't have to keep flying the wrong way. No matter what the mistake, God will forgive you and turn you around.

An Example to Consider: Gideon

Read Judges 6:8.

At the point that we meet Gideon in this chapter of the Bible, his people had forsaken God. God had rescued them from slavery in Egypt, compassionately provided for all of their needs, brought them into the Promised Land, and loved them deeply. But they didn't appreciate all that God did, and they were not faithful to the God who was faithful to them. Instead, they began to worship other gods. God was disappointed and hurt, and for a while, He let them go their own way and do their own thing. Without God to lead and defend them, the Israelites were easily defeated by their enemies. Other countries came in and ravaged their land and all that they owned. When they were doing well, they called on other gods; but now that they were in trouble, they knew that only *their* God, the God whom they had forsaken, could help them. In response to their cries, God appointed Gideon as the one who would deliver the Israelites from their enemies.

When the Lord told Gideon why He was there, we find Gideon's response in Judges 6:15: "'Pardon me, my lord,' Gideon replied, 'but how can I save Israel? My clan is the weakest in Manasseh, and I am the least in my family.'" Gideon was apparently the least of the least, but God chose him. And notice how God first addressed Gideon. Judges 6:12 says, "When the angel of the Lord appeared to Gideon, he said, 'The Lord is with you, mighty warrior.'" Gideon saw himself as the least of the least, but God knew what He could make of him, so He called him by what He saw: "mighty warrior." Gideon saw himself in the *now*; God saw him in the *not yet*. When Gideon was willing to let go of his own negative self-image and to let God make of him whatever God chose, Gideon was used by God to bring victory to Israel.

Dear God,

You know that—in spite of how I act and what I say to others—deep inside I feel like Gideon. I feel like the least of the least. There's nothing good in me, God. I'm a failure to you, my family, and myself. I can't see how You could possibly do anything good with me. But reading the story of Gideon gives me hope. If You saw a mighty warrior in a man who had nothing and was nothing, then maybe You can see something in me, too. God, help me to see what You see. Help me to know what You want me to do. Don't let me miss my destiny, my calling. Deliver me, God, from myself and all those around me who detract from my serving You fully. Open my eyes. Open my ears. Let me see You and hear Your voice. Speak, Lord, because, more than any other time in my life, I am listening. I love you. Amen.

CHAPTER 7

Help a Brother Out

While I was at the window of my house,

looking through the curtain,

I saw some naive young men,

and one in particular who lacked common sense.

Proverbs 7:6-7 NLT

You Are Your Brother's Brother

I have four sons. I considered it the responsibility of the older brothers to help reinforce the teaching of their father to their younger brothers. They had been with me longer. They knew me better. They knew what I felt about certain things, what I had taught them about various matters. I expected my older sons to tell their brothers just what they had heard me say. I didn't expect them to hear one thing from me and then pass along a contradictory message to their brothers.

Son, I urge you today to pass along to your brothers what you have heard from your heavenly Father. No matter how long you have been in a personal relationship with Him, there is always another brother who hasn't known Him as long or doesn't know Him as well. God considers it your responsibility to help reinforce His Word among your brothers.

Genesis 4 tells us the story of how Cain killed his brother Abel. In Genesis 4:9, God asked him after he committed his crime, "Where is your brother Abel?" He arrogantly and impudently replied, "I don't know. Am I my brother's keeper?" Just because he asked that question, it does not mean that the right answer was "yes," as many people assume. If God had responded to Cain's question, the answer would have been, "No, you are not your brother's keeper. You are your brother's brother."

Animals in zoos have keepers. Human beings should never have keepers. Keepers are hired for their positions. Brothers are born into theirs. A human being decides who will be a keeper. God decides who will be brothers. Abel did not need Cain to be his "keeper," but he did need him to be his brother. No man or boy you know needs a keeper, but they all need a brother.

Watch Out for the Younger Ones

In Joliet, Illinois, a mother was in the backyard with her two sons—a two-year-old and a nine- year-old. They were playing and having a good time. The mother went back into the house for just a few minutes. When she came back out, she didn't see her two-year-old son. She looked at the older son and asked, "Where is your brother?" He replied nonchalantly, "I don't know." The mother just knew in that instant that the younger brother had jumped into the swimming pool. She ran to the pool, and to her chagrin, she found her young child floating face-down on top of the water. He had drowned.

Immediately she pulled him out. She had been trained in CPR, so she began applying CPR to the child, but he was not responding. Her other son said, "Momma, you're not doing it right." He pushed her out of the way, began doing CPR on his little brother, and was able to bring him back to life. The nine-year-old became a hero and was acknowledged by the national news because he took responsibility for his little brother.

Son, you may not be acknowledged in the news, but you can become every bit a hero by rescuing a brother from danger or death. It doesn't take long for a brother to wander off and fall—or even jump into some trouble and get himself into a mess. Nobody's looking, so the brother really has no idea how deep this pit is. Before he knows it, he finds himself in over his head and sinking into a dead situation. We need some older brothers who have spent some time in the presence of God to go look for their brothers and rescue them. If a young boy can breathe life back into a two-year-old, how much more can the Spirit of God, coming forth through an older brother, breathe life back into a brother who has become spiritually dead!

Keep the Curtains Open

The Scripture text for this chapter begins, "While I was at the window of my house, looking through the curtain . . ." This brother wasn't hanging out in the streets. He had found his way home. He was inside, safe and secure. But even though he had found his place, he was looking out for other young men who were still wandering around in the streets. In the same way, we need to look out for our little brothers, whether the age gap between us is great or negligible. We always need to guard against getting ourselves inside to safety, but then forgetting about those who are still outside dealing with all of the temptations—still feeling alone and vulnerable. We always need to remember where we've come from and that we have a responsibility for those coming along behind us.

When you keep your curtains open and you are looking out for younger brothers, you remember when you had no sense, when you were way out there, when you were in trouble. You never want to forget the place from where God has brought you. You've got to keep the curtains open.

Some people don't have curtains on their windows; they only have blinds. If that is true for you, keep in mind that when you pull the blinds down, the world outside is *blind* to what you are doing inside, but you are also blind to all that is going on outside. Don't become blind to the world; there are people in the world who need you.

Know What Year It Is

Keeping your eyes open and remembering where you've come from will also keep you relevant enough to reach a brother when he needs you. You can't live in the past. You have to stay up with the times in order to know what our young people are coming to grips with whenever they are outside. You need to know the current issues and temptations they're facing because they aren't the same ones you experienced when you were growing up.

There are several versions of a new television commercial that shows a slightly older child telling younger siblings how different TV-watching is today from the time he or she was growing up (no more than four or five years earlier). The child is pontificating about how much better the younger children have it today with easy access to so many different channels, multiple viewing options, and portability of the TV screen. And, of course, the younger children are rolling their eyes and tuning out. If we aren't careful, that's what will happen when we start talking with young people about life issues. Instead of starting with the tired phrase, "When I was your age," we need to understand what life is like for young people today—and start there.

We need to recognize that the temptations and trials we faced, while they seemed difficult in that day, are nothing in comparison to what young people are facing today. When I think about my own life, I recall that I didn't really leave my neighborhood until I finished high school. It wasn't until I got to college that my world grew larger and I began to realize how much more was out there. In contrast, young people today can go around the world without ever leaving their laptop. When I was growing up, we had three channels on our TV, and they went off the air around midnight. My kids can't believe there was a time of day when the TV channels went off the air. This is a different time and a different day, so we have to stay relevant.

Go Look for the Lost

I know, however, why some brothers don't want to look outside. For some, if they are not careful, looking out will mess up their outlook (their attitude, their viewpoint, their perception). They are tired of hearing about murders, shootings, disasters, drug addictions, people being jailed and all that. But, rather than allowing what you're looking at to affect your outlook, I would suggest letting your outlook help you overcome what you're looking at. You know that your outlook is good because you were able to get out of the streets, get out of poverty, and get out of sin. You know what Jesus can do. You know what the power of the Holy Spirit can do. So take that outlook and go look out for a brother.

The need outside can seem overwhelming. The person at the window didn't have to look around to find this group. He simply looked out, and there was this bunch of naïve young men—immature, inexperienced, and adolescent. Watching them, he could see that they were filled with nonsense, talking as though they knew it all when, in actuality, they knew nothing about life. They were behaving like children, not like men.

And in the midst of all of them, there was one who stood out above the rest. He stood out because he had no sense at all. He was the type of person about whom one might say, "He doesn't have the sense to come in out of the rain." It's one thing to operate in nonsense—to be seventeen years old and talking as if you know more than everybody in the world. That's nonsense. To think you're going to be successful without education or training—that's nonsense. To think you're a man because of how many women you've slept with—that's nonsense. To get a woman pregnant, but not be willing to father that child—that's nonsense.

No Sense of Direction

Yet there's a difference between nonsense and no sense. You can tell the one brother had no sense because of his direction, his position, and the fact that he was operating in darkness. Proverbs 7:8-9 (NLT) says, "He was crossing the street near the house of an immoral woman, strolling down the path by her house. It was at twilight, in the evening, as deep darkness fell." You can always tell a person with no sense.

Notice first his sense of direction. He was crossing the street to go down the path by the house of an immoral woman. That was the *wrong* direction. Son, when you think about the direction you are going, ask yourself, *If I keep going this direction for the next five years, where am I going to end up?* The answer to that is that you will have gone deeper in the same direction you are going now. You can't think that you are doing drugs, drinking, watching porn, and having premarital sex now, but in five years, you'll suddenly come out on the other side. There is no other side. You will find yourself in so deep that it will be harder, much harder, to ever come back out. If you are going in the direction of God, family, service, and community, in five years you will be deeper in all of those areas. But if you are going in the direction of sin, you will be deeper into the sin. That's why we need older brothers to watch out for the younger brothers.

Strolling in Darkness

Look again at where this young man positioned himself. He was "strolling down the path by her house." This was not an accidental situation. He crossed the street to get nearer the house of the immoral woman. And he didn't run by. He didn't rush by. He didn't walk quickly by. No, he *strolled* down the path by her house. He wanted to be sure she would see him. He positioned himself for sin.

Notice the fact that this man was operating under the shield of darkness. He began strolling past this woman's house at twilight. That was at dusk—at the very last moments before it became totally dark. He had obviously timed this. He wanted her to be able to see him, but then he wanted it to be dark for the rest of the time he was with her. Keep in mind, too, that the darkness there and then was not like the darkness here and now. There were no street lights. There was nothing but the moon to give any hint at all of light on the situation. This man was hiding his intentions and his deeds in the darkness. As Solomon said, this is a brother with no sense. He could be living in the light of God, enjoying fellowship with the Lord; but instead, he is creeping around in the dark, seeking sin.

We need brothers who will be looking out for this young man, confronting him, and letting him know he is headed in the wrong direction and needs to turn around. He is too weak in himself to get out of this situation on his own. He needs the strength of a brother to help him find his way home.

Broken, But Still Running

In the 2012 Olympics in London, Manteo Mitchell ran the 4x400m relay. He was supposed to take the baton, run around the track, and hand the baton off to the next runner. But when he was about halfway around the track, he said he felt something that he knew wasn't right. The more he ran, the more it hurt. But he kept running until he finished his portion of the race. After it was all over, his leg was x-rayed, and he discovered he had broken his leg at the 200m mark. In spite of a painful broken leg, he kept running. He said later that he knew he had to keep running because what he did wouldn't affect only him, but the entire team as well. The other young men on the team had trained hard and put forth so much effort. If he didn't fulfill his commitment, he would be dashing their dreams as well as his.

He realized later on what had happened. A couple days prior to this, Mitchell fell down some stairs in the Olympic village. It was the fall from his past that caused him to be broken in the present. But even though he was broken, he kept running because he knew that there were other men who would not get to the next level until he passed on to them what they needed—the baton.

Son, you may be one of the broken older brothers. You may have fallen in the past and you are broken in the present. So, you may be using this as the reason why you can't care for anyone else. You're too broken to minister to others. You may be broken financially, relationally, emotionally, or in a variety of ways. But you need to know that every now and then, God allows for us to be broken to arrange it so that we can be a blessing. But we've got to keep running in our brokenness so that we can help a little brother who needs what it is that we have to offer.

Speak Out!

We also need some big brothers who are willing to speak out to a little brother. Why? Read Proverbs 7:10-20 (NLT):

> The woman approached him,
> seductively dressed and sly of heart.

She was the brash, rebellious type,

> never content to stay at home.

She is often in the streets and markets,

> soliciting at every corner.

She threw her arms around him and kissed him,

> and with a brazen look she said,

"I've just made my peace offerings

> and fulfilled my vows.

You're the one I was looking for!

> I came out to find you, and here you are!

My bed is spread with beautiful blankets,

> with colored sheets of Egyptian linen.

I've perfumed my bed

> with myrrh, aloes, and cinnamon.

Come, let's drink our fill of love until morning.

> Let's enjoy each other's caresses,

for my husband is not home.

> He's away on a long trip.

He has taken a wallet full of money with him

> and won't return until later this month."

This foolish little brother is about to get into a situation that he can't handle. We've got to speak out. Homeboy is already headed in the wrong direction, positioning himself in the wrong place, and operating in darkness. Now here comes the wrong woman. He's about to get into trouble. He's about to experience some consequences for his wrong actions because he has no character. That is because he has received no counsel. Nobody has sat him down and explained to him the consequences of his behavior and actions. Nobody has ever warned him about women like this.

If we give our brothers wise counsel from the Word of God, they will develop Christian character, and the consequences will take care of themselves. Otherwise, they will be headed in the wrong direction, and along will come the wrong woman.

Deception Is Attractive

When we look at the woman in this chapter, we see that she is especially deceptive. She isn't a prostitute by profession, but she appears dressed like one. She is actually the wife of a wealthy man. We know that because she speaks of her beautiful blankets and colorful sheets made of Egyptian linen. And she mentions that her husband took "a wallet full of money" with him when he left on his long trip.

So why would a woman married to a wealthy, influential man who gives her beautiful things want to hook up with a young fool who has nothing? At least part of that answer is found in verses 11 and 12: "She was the brash, rebellious type, never content to stay at home. She is often in the streets and markets, soliciting at every corner." There was something in this woman's heart that wasn't right. She was restless, "never content to stay at home." She was brash and rebellious. It didn't matter how much her husband gave her or did for her, her heart didn't appreciate him.

But it is also very possible that this husband was reaping his own consequences even in his marriage. He probably was once attracted to this "feisty" woman who was beautiful and who fed his ego. She made him feel that he was so special. She probably told him the same thing she said to this young man: "You're the one I was looking for! I came out to find you, and here you are!" He was taken in by her sly ways and entered into a lifetime relationship with her. Now he is paying the consequences by living with an unpleasant, unfaithful wife.

This young man she is approaching is no match for this woman who is used to getting what she wants. He has no common sense, so he doesn't stop to ask himself why she looks like a hooker when she is actually a married woman. He doesn't stop to ask himself why, instead of saying hello and introducing herself, she immediately throws her arms around him and kisses him. Just as Judas misused a kiss to betray Jesus, this woman also misuses a kiss to seduce this foolish young man.

Her behavior is so blatant. She begins with the physical—arousing him with her seductive dress and her kisses. Then she pretends to have a religious side by telling him that she has just come from the temple, where she has made peace offerings. Then she moves into her sexual proposition, telling him how sweet her bed is. And then she mentions the financial side, letting him know that her husband has lots of money. She is telling him everything he wants to hear, but he doesn't have enough common sense to recognize she is just using him.

He doesn't know enough to realize that this is the time to run. He doesn't see himself like an ox on the way to slaughter, like a bird approaching a snare. He doesn't see himself like a fly that is about to be caught up in a spider's web. Where are you, big brother? You've got to go talk to him. You've got to keep him from getting caught. You've got to tell him like it is. You've encountered women like this before. You know what this one's like. You know what she's doing. Warn him. Stop him. Counsel him. Turn the brother around.

There's Always a Way of Escape

A brother needs to know that God can keep him from being entrapped. He needs to hear 1 Corinthians 10:13: "No temptation has overtaken you except what is common to mankind. And God is faithful; he will not let you be tempted beyond what you can bear. But when you are tempted, he will also provide a way out so that you can endure it." You need to let him know that the only reason you are in church, serving God and walking the right direction is because God gave you a way of escape. It wasn't that you were never tempted. It wasn't that you never saw something that you wanted, but you knew it wasn't for you.

Let the brother know that when he received Jesus into his life, the Holy Spirit came to reside within him and to strengthen him. (See

Ephesians 3:16.) He needs to know that Jesus gives him strength. (See 1 Timothy 1:12.) He needs to know that he does not have to get caught in a trap that the enemy sets for him. Second Timothy 2:25-26 tells us the importance of offering counsel: "Opponents must be gently instructed, in the hope that God will grant them repentance leading them to a knowledge of the truth, and that they will come to their senses and escape from the trap of the devil, who has taken them captive to do his will." This young brother needs to come to his senses and escape the trap set for him. Don't let him down, older brother.

Fooled by the Temporary

Now, some of us don't understand why a young man is even in a situation to be tempted. We wonder why he doesn't just stay away from that corner. We wonder why he doesn't just avoid women like the woman in this chapter. The reason is that he is tempted by the temporary. In this case, this woman was offering to share her beautiful bed with him, to make love to him, and to do all of this without any expectations, without any long-term ties. She told him that her husband was away, but he would be coming back later in the month. This let him know she was not asking him to enter into a permanent relationship. She would not be expecting him to change his life for her or make any commitment to her. This was a *temporary* situation—a *temporary* opportunity to fulfill his lusts. It appeals to

256

him because he thinks he can just do something that feels good to him and then be on his way with no consequences or repercussions.

Younger brother doesn't understand the way the enemy operates. The enemy takes what we think is temporary and makes it permanent. Dr. A. Louis Patterson, my mentor, has said that, "A little pleasure leads to perpetual ongoing pain." Conversely, he says, "A little pain leads to perpetual ongoing pleasure." Think about it. This woman is offering him pure pleasure. If it weren't pleasurable, it wouldn't tempt him. And this isn't just having sex with *any* woman. This is a woman who has made herself beautiful, who comes onto him in a very sensual way, who can take him into a lovely, romantic setting that is probably nicer than his own home. Having sex with *this* woman wouldn't just feed his lust, it would feed his ego, too. He could go around telling his male friends who he was able to get. He would have multiplied pleasure.

Gain from Pain

If he walks away from that temptation, it is going to be painful. This brother *wants* what she has to offer. He has already been aroused. He is already feeling something in his body. All systems are go. For him to walk away at this point, he knows it's going to hurt. But what he has to know is that the pain he will experience would only be temporary. It wouldn't last. He wouldn't feel that way always. That feeling will go away. But that temporary pain would have led to ongoing pleasure. He would have the pleasure of knowing that he didn't commit adultery with another man's wife. He will have the pleasure of knowing that he is a man of integrity. He will have the pleasure of self-respect.

If he doesn't walk away from that temptation, he may experience a night of pleasure, but the pain could last for the rest of his life. My grandmother says, "Two minutes of pleasure can lead to eighteen years of pain." A man can enjoy a night of pleasure with a woman, but spend the next eighteen or more years supporting the child that was born as a result of that one night of pleasure.

It may not even be caring for the child that is the problem. He may not even *like* the woman he was with, and now he has to put up with her calls, her expectations, and her demands until that child becomes an adult. And, even if he loves his child, it isn't a normal relationship. A man in a long black robe sitting behind a tall desk has told him how often he can see his child, where to pick him up, how long he can spend with him, who else can be there, and where he gets to take him. That same judge has also informed him about how much money he must give to the support of his child, even though he has no practical voice regarding how that money is spent. He enjoyed his eighteen minutes of pleasure, but now he'll be paying a painful price for the rest of his life. We need some big brothers to speak up because our young brothers are tempted by the temporary.

Attracted to Dysfunction

The young man in this story is also tempted by the unordinary—the out of the ordinary. Notice I did not say "extraordinary." As a sidebar here, let me address the meaning of words. I believe we should call something what it is. Some men, in an effort to make their sin seem not so terrible, will say to someone, "I've gotten caught up in an extramarital affair." That doesn't sound so bad. He was "caught up," which sounds like it wasn't really his fault. And it's an "extra" relationship that is simply in addition to his relationship with his wife; it isn't as though he has left his wife for another woman. Wait a minute! Adultery is adultery no matter what euphemism someone uses to try to make it seem not so bad. If he wants to make a confession, the man should say, "I have committed adultery," and not try to make it sound like anything other than the sin that it is.

There was nothing extraordinary about what this woman was offering this young man, but it was certainly out of the ordinary. It was a dysfunctional proposition. She was not behaving as a wife and homemaker would normally behave. Rather than stay in her home at night, she was out on the street seducing a young man. If she were dressing provocatively for her husband and behaving in a seductive manner to let him know that she was going to give him some pleasure that night, there would be nothing wrong with that—and a lot of things right about it. But she wasn't doing this for her husband. She was behaving this way for a fool. When her

259

husband was home, she wasn't doing any of this. But in his absence, she was making a fool of herself by seducing a fool. There was something very dysfunctional in her behavior, but it was also very attractive to this young man.

Big Brother, Where Are You?

Where is the big brother that should be watching out for this young man? Where is the big brother who can talk to him about pain and pleasure? Where is the big brother who can tell him that the temptation is only temporary, but the consequences will be perpetual? Where is the big brother who can let him know that God's got something better in store for him? Where is the big brother who is willing to speak up to try to bring him to his senses?

Even as you are reading this, you may be thinking about someone for whom you feel this sense of responsibility. Maybe he is a younger brother in terms of physical age. Perhaps he is simply less mature than you, or maybe he is younger in Christ, (he hasn't been a Christian as long as you). At any rate, you need to be making a difference in another brother's life. You don't have to wait until you can get a group together, start a nonprofit, or do something on a large scale. Find one man or boy to whom you are willing to be a brother and begin to be there for him—love, encourage, counsel and support him. If everyone would reach one, then everyone would be reached. Find the one to whom God would lead you.

You may argue, "If I help just one person, that's not going to make a difference." But it *will* make a difference. God's Word always makes a difference. If you say to him the same thing the Lord is saying, it *will* make a difference. There is power in the Word. If you are walking with God today, it is because somebody spoke a word to you. Somebody took time to share the Word of God with you. Somebody cared enough to stop you from ruining your life by introducing you to the God who spoke the Word.

Just Say the Word

Matthew 8:5-8 tells this story:

> When Jesus had entered Capernaum, a centurion came to him, asking for help. "Lord," he said, "my servant lies at home paralyzed, suffering terribly." Jesus said to him, "Shall I come and heal him?" The centurion replied, "Lord, I do not deserve to have you come under my roof. But just say the word, and my servant will be healed."

That's how powerful the word is that comes from Jesus. Jesus didn't even have to go to where the person was. He just had to say the word, wherever He was, and it would be done. The story concludes, "Then Jesus said to the centurion, 'Go! Let it be done just as you believed it would.' And his servant was healed at that moment" (v. 13). The servant was healed when Jesus spoke the word.

If you want to know when the man or boy in your life will get up, when he will be healed spiritually and emotionally, and when he will go to another level, it is when you speak a word from the Scriptures to him. There is power in the Word of God!

Life in a Word World

Once when I went to Daytona Beach to preach a series of meetings for Bishop Derek Triplett at Hope Fellowship Church, the evening service began with music and worship, someone gave a testimony, and then I preached. The third and final night I was there, a young woman gave her testimony. She began to talk about the goodness of God, and of Jesus Christ, His Son. She talked about what God had done for her, how much the church meant to her, and what a blessing the pastor was to her and her family. She shared that she was a homemaker and has a fine husband.

She said that when her husband goes to work, she and her three-year-old son watch a show together on PBS called "WordWorld." I had watched a lot of PBS shows with my own children as they were growing up, but I hadn't heard of that one. She shared that in "WordWorld," the characters spell out a word, and when they do, the word actually *becomes* what they have spelled out. So, if the characters spell "ball"—b-a-l-l—they spell it and speak it, and the word becomes a ball. If they spell b-a-t, then the word becomes a bat. When they spell it and speak it, it becomes what they have spoken.

What I am trying to tell you is that we live in a "word world." If you can speak the word, the word becomes what you speak. Romans 4:17 refers to "the God who . . . calls into being things that were not." Proverbs 18:21 (KJV) says, "Death and life are in the power of the tongue." There is power in the words we speak!

One of our problems is that we only know how to spell little words: ball, bat, and car. We need to learn to spell some big words: emancipation, salvation, liberation, freedom, overcoming addictions, healthy relationships, good marriages, manhood, fatherhood, etc. We need to spell some big words because we have a big God who can make them come to pass. This is a word world in which we live.

Pull 'Em Out

Not only do we older brothers need to look out for the younger brothers, keep free from the lures of the world, and speak out to the brothers, but also we need to pull them out. These younger brothers aren't able to get out by themselves. In the verses from Proverbs 7, it is as if this woman has a trap set for him. She looks and speaks to him in a beguiling, seductive way. The enemy has a trap set for him. She tells him how beautiful her house is, but verse 27 (NLT) says, "Her house is the road to the grave. Her bedroom is the den of death." The previous verse says that "many men have been her victims." Tragically, verse 22 says, "He followed her at once, like an ox going to the slaughter." He went in, but we never read that he ever came out. Her house was his road to the grave. Without any sense to guide him, he was deceived by the woman's beauty, speech, and promises, and he became "like an ox going to the slaughter."

Son, there are some houses you can go into and never come out. I'm not trying to keep you from living or having fun. I just know—because I've lived longer and have experienced more than you—that certain houses will lead you to death and destruction. Some people with whom I went to high school went into a drug house and never came out. Family members who went into a whorehouse disappeared. Some people who went into a bar, a house of alcohol, never escaped alcoholism. These "houses" are roads to the grave. You can go in spiritually and emotionally healthy, but your spirit dies in those kinds of houses.

Don't Be a Hypocrite

What really got to me as I read this chapter of Proverbs is that Solomon sat in his house watching all of this, but he did nothing to help the brother out. He saw what was happening. He saw the young man walking down the street and crossing over to the woman's house. He watched her come out, observed the seduction scene, and saw him go in like an ox going to the slaughter, but he did nothing! Also, Solomon couldn't have heard from his window what that woman was saying, and he couldn't have known what was in her house, if he hadn't heard and seen all of that for himself at some time. He experienced all of that himself one day when *he* was the foolish young man walking down the street without any sense, not knowing any better than to let himself be seduced by this woman. Solomon may be sounding so holy and spiritual as he points out the folly of this young man for what he does, but he wasn't so spiritual when *he* was the one going down that street.

You and I know about what some shameful things look like, not because of some spiritual insight we have, but because we were there ourselves. We know from our own experience what it was like. We also know how hard it is to get out. It isn't a matter of not having an option for getting out. It's that we can't get out on our own. In our past situation we didn't get out on our own. We needed someone to help us get out. Now *we* need to be those big brothers who will help other brothers out. We need to go after those men and boys when we see them walking in the wrong direction. We need to call to them, show up in front of them, and go in after them, if we must, to help them get out before they die in those houses.

Reach Back and Give Them Jesus

In the movie *The Dark Knight Rises*, Bruce Wayne gets thrown into an underground prison. He is lowered down on a rope, like a bucket being lowered into a well. The rope is pulled up, and he's trapped in there. There are no guards needed since there's no possibility of escape. The prisoners have come up with their own governing system—their own rules, boundaries, and standards. They're all there for life, so they call their prison "Hell."

Bruce Wayne finds himself in Hell, but in his heart he decides that he isn't like the rest of the prisoners; so he wants to find a way to get out. He tries to climb out and gets up so far, but falls back down. He tries again and climbs a little higher than before, but still falls down. He tries again and again. The other prisoners watching encourage him. They pat him on the back and tell him he can do it, and they're clapping for him as he rises a little higher and a little higher. I love the attitude of the other prisoners. They aren't trying to pull him back into their mess. Instead, they're cheering him on. They feel that even if they can't get out of Hell themselves, they can at least be happy for someone else who does.

Finally, Bruce Wayne—being Batman, the superhero that he is—makes it out! He looks back down into the pit, and the other prisoners are applauding him. Then, one of my favorite parts in the movie happens. Bruce Wayne is now free. He's ready to head back to Gotham, back to his mansion, his fortune, and his comfortable lifestyle. But just before walking away from the pit, he throws the rope back down to the others. He understands that what he has just gotten out of, other men are still trapped in. He knows that he has gotten out, but others are still there and have no hope of escape. So he turns around and does something to help them get out, too.

Dr. Freddie Haynes, pastor of Friendship-West Baptist Church in Dallas, says, "When you overcome, you've got to help somebody else to come on over." Son, when God has pulled you out of something, you've got to reach back and help someone else out. God sent Jesus down to rescue us. Jesus was like a rope of love that God threw around the world so that we would have Someone to hang onto—and Someone to pull us out.

Now, we have to turn around and do for others what God has done for us. We have to give them Jesus. We may feel tired after all we've been through. We may feel that we're broken and have no strength left, but there are others still in Hell and we are free. We have no choice. We have to reach back. We have to let them know that the same One who brought us out will bring them out, too. How can we go to heaven alone? How can we break God's heart by not loving others as He has loved us? We've got to reach back and help a brother out!

An Example to Consider: Joseph

Please open your Bible and read Genesis 37:39-47.

The story of Joseph demonstrates the contention that a father can introduce into a family when he favors one child over another. Genesis 37:3-4 clearly says, "Now Israel loved Joseph more than any of his other sons, because he had been born to him in his old age; and he made an ornate robe for him. When his brothers saw that their father loved him more than any of them, they hated him and could not speak a kind word to him." Joseph didn't help matters by arrogantly telling his brothers about his dreams that they would someday bow down to him. One day when they were away from home, the angry brothers sold Joseph as a slave to some travelers, and then told their father that he had been killed by wild animals.

Years later Joseph had an opportunity to take revenge on his brothers. Through a series of God-ordained circumstances, Joseph had transitioned from being a slave in a dungeon to become a leader in Egypt. There was a famine in Egypt and surrounding lands as well. The brothers had to come to Joseph to ask for grain so that they wouldn't die. Even though they didn't recognize him, Joseph knew who they were. Here was his chance to get revenge. But the years that Joseph had suffered in slavery and prison had changed him. He was no longer the same arrogant person he once was. When he saw his brothers, he didn't want to retaliate; he wanted to help them. Rather than killing, imprisoning, or enslaving them, he gave them food, invited them to live in Egypt for the duration of the famine, and sent them home to bring his beloved father to him.

Time passed. When their father died, they feared that Joseph would now turn on them, but he said, "'You intended to harm me, but God intended it for good to accomplish what is now being done, the saving of many lives. So then, don't be afraid. I will provide for you and your children.' And he reassured them and spoke kindly to them" (Genesis 50:20-21). He had a chance to let his brothers experience the hell they had put him through, but because of God's love and grace, he chose instead to help his brothers out.

Dear God,

I realize that I have been more concerned for myself than for others. While there are brothers all around me who need help, I focus on myself and what will please me. Please forgive me, Lord. Give me Your heart for the men around me who are lost and headed for hell—whether it be a hell here on earth or an eternity without You. Grant me wisdom to know how to speak out to them, courage to reach out to them, and strength to pull them out of the messes they are in. Give me the grace and love You gave to Joseph, which allowed him to love even those brothers who had wounded and abused him. Let me love them as Jesus loves me, and let me be a brother to my brothers. Amen.